# JOE PATERNO
## THE COACH FROM BYZANTIUM

BY
GEORGE PATERNO

SPORTS PUBLISHING
AN IMPRINT OF SAGAMORE PUBLISHING
CHAMPAIGN, IL

Director of Production: Susan M. McKinney
Dustjacket design: Julie Denzer

ISBN: 1-57167-153-6


SPORTS PUBLISHING
a division of
Sagamore Publishing
804 N. Neil
Champaign, IL 61820
www.sagamorepub.com

Printed in the United States

*To three noble friends:*

Friend and father, Angelo Lafayette Paterno
Friend and priest, Thomas V. Birmingham S.J.
Friend and teacher, Terrance J. Rafferty

# CONTENTS

# ACKNOWLEDGMENTS

The author gives thanks to all the people who have been part of Joe Paterno's saga for just being there. All of Joe's friends, assistant coaches and administrative staff individually and together contributed to the events that have led to his success.

I'm also very thankful to Sagamore Publishing for giving me an opportunity to tell my story. The suggestions and editing skills of Mike Pearson and Susan McKinney helped me learn a new craft.

The entire PSU Sports Information Department; Bud Thalman, Jeff Nelson, Frank Giardenia and their staff, happily provided dates and statistics.

When I was discouraged, an old Pt. Washington nice guy, Paul Nussolese, prodded me on to tell people what Joe meant to him.

I am especially indebted to my former pupil, dear friend John Dockery and his wife, Ann, whose endorsement encouraged me to finish the book and seek a publisher. My thanks to Ann Fitzgerald who devotedly transcribed my tapes and assembled all the data for the manuscript.

To everyone, thank you.

# PREFACE

Many people have asked me why I wrote this book. My answer would have to be that I had a story to tell that I felt poignantly relates to the average American family.

Both Joe and I were fortunate to have a wonderful and understanding father. My book is a family continuum to the speech he made in 1945 as Director of Interfaith Movement Inc. Dad's following speech is the format that became seminal to the character of Joe Paterno and what he stands for and has tried to achieve through football.

*Remarks of Hon. Angelo Paterno*
*Clerk of the Supreme Court of the First Judicial District*
*and Director of Interfaith Movement, Inc.*
*Thursday, October 25, 1945 at the Barbizon-Plaza Hotel*

Realizing that the program for the evening is quite lengthy, I do not propose to take one minute longer than is absolutely necessary for me to convey to you assembled here this evening my thoughts in reference to this worthy Interfaith Movement.

Interfaith has been construed in diverse ways. Some people look upon the Movement as an outlet for prodigious writings wherein they extol the virtues of our cause; others expound the theories of Interfaith by loquacious and lengthy discourses; and some utilize a combination of both.

To me, Interfaith has only one meaning. To me, it signifies the opportunity to manifest our consideration for our fellow beings by our conduct. All of the talking and all of the literature in behalf of tolerance are wasted energies unless accompanied by some overt acts of the proponent in furtherance of our principles. Unless the individual by his personal conduct in his every day life profess the sincerity of his teachings, no one will be impressed. One cannot proclaim his affection for a person of another faith or color, and then refuse that person admission to his society because he does not worship in the same church or because he happened to be born of colored parents. A person should mean what he says or else he should refrain from comment. That type of individual is the bigot upon whom we must concentrate our efforts. He must be educated to the fallacy of his conduct by the example that we, of Interfaith Movement, set by our individual acts.

My forebears have passed on to me a heritage. This treasured heritage had been thundered down through the ages to them, and they have kept it by their exemplary lives. That heritage, ladies and gentlemen, is the will to do unto others as you would want them to do unto you.

Stripped of all descriptive phrases and divested of its many interpretations, Interfaith means just that: Do unto others as you would want them to do unto you. This Movement should emanate from our hearts. The propelling force will then be strong enough to enable us to overcome all the obstacles placed in our paths. We must have unity of thought. We must have unity of action. We must all act as missionaries and we must preach to our fellow men, night and day, of the evils of this hydrated monster of bigotry. The forces of intolerance and hate are on the march today. The seed of hate and discord is being sown all around us. It is our task to inculcate our worthy ideals into the warped minds of the weakling before this seed takes root.

The echo of the thundering guns has scarcely subsided, leaving us to the sad memories of the flower of our American youth who will never return to their loved ones. A mighty armada of naval might is now assembling in our harbor. From the largest to the smallest vessel in that fleet, fresh from mortal combat with our common enemies, there is written in their battle histories countless exhibitions of Interfaith. There was no discrimination in our armed forces. They fought and died to perpetuate the ideals for which we assembled here tonight, for which we stand, and for which we will continue to fight.

As we leave this assembly hall tonight, let us all make a solemn pledge to the thousands of American youth, white and black, Protestant, Catholic and Jew, who have made the supreme sacrifice, that we will carry on those ideas for which they paid so dearly. They died that we might live and enjoy the benefits of this great and glorious country.

In conclusion, let me urge you who are assembled here this evening to rededicate your lives to the proposition that all of the forces of intolerance must be expunged from our midst and that you will become a crusader in this most worthy cause.

# FOREWORD

As an awkward, impressionable teenage runningback at Brooklyn Prep High School in the early sixties, even I knew there was something very different about my coach, George Paterno. His tough-guy reputation as a Marine, a New York City detective, and a football star at Brown had preceded him, but what I was not ready for on that first day of summer practice was a philosopher coach who quoted the classics for motivation. "Ball carriers should run with the fearless abandon of Achilles and the quiet cunning of Odysseus". I didn't realize that a literary reference guide would be a necessary addendum to my football playbook, but I did know that George Paterno, like his older brother Joe was not your ordinary football coach and not your ordinary guy from Brooklyn.

His famous brother, Joe Paterno, is the stuff of legend—a Hall of Fame coach, the winningest football coach in Division I, a prominent figure at a major university for three decades, with couple of national championship to his credit. But Joe Paterno is even more than a very successful person in a tough profession. He is an intelligent, educated, moral man who cares deeply about family, country, morality, and kids learning about life through a demanding game. Joe Paterno will just as quickly quote Robert Browning as Vince Lombardi, urging a player to fulfill his potential, reminding him that "his reach should exceed his grasp." Joe Paterno is almost an anachronism, swimming against the tide in a time when today's athletic arena is populated by selfish, greedy players, behaving outrageously to promote their own ends. Joe Paterno is a voice of reason in a sporting world gone mad, but even so, he is far from perfect, a fact his brother shares with us.

In *Joe Paterno: The Coach From Byzantium,* George Paterno gives us an honest, human view of his famous brother, struggling with his own personal pressures of family, career, and the shifting landscape of big-time college football. George Paterno also shares with us his own anguish of living in the shadow of his celebrity brother and trying to decide whether to compete with or to support his older sibling.

George Paterno's personal portrait of his legendary brother answers that question in honest, raw detail. *Joe Paterno: The Coach From Byzantium* also reminds us once again that modern day sports heroes like Michael Jordan, Cal Ripken, Jr., and Joe Paterno are not mythical figures descended from Mount Olympus, but rather mere mortals with feet of clay like the rest of us.

John Dockery

# Chapter One

# FAMILY ROOTS

Most people know about the Roman Empire which lasted about 400 years. Few know about the Byzantine Empire that lasted over one thousand years. When Emperor Constantine moved the capital to Byzantium, and named it Constantinople, now Istanbul, Christianity flourished. The mix of Asia Minor and new groups foreign to Rome created a melange of religions, races and ethnic groups that produced a unique power structure. Constantine was followed by Theodosius and Justin (who wanted to rebuild the Roman Empire). They developed the basis of the Christian world. The Eastern Empire was dominated by Greek culture, but was influenced by the Persians, The Arabs, the Balkans, and even western Russia, and then eventually fell to the Ottoman Turks, whose influence was also reflected in the Empire.

A true Byzantine is involved in Christian mysticism, in visible and abstract good and evil, and in the supernatural. Byzantium was truly a bridge between antiquity and the modern world; enshrouded in mystery, with survival based on intrigue. Only a brilliant mind capable of intellectual compassion and Machiavellian reality joined with personal ambition could rise to greatness. To maintain dignity and Christian ideals among so many threatening cultures, (including Rome), a

Byzantine person had to live by his intellect, and if he wanted to advance in society he had to have a plan. Joe Paterno is that kind of man.

If ever there was a peripatetic surname, "Paterno" would be one. With lineage traces from Hellenistic Macedonian to Turkish Byzantium, to Albania, Calabria and on to Sicily where they first established a city that produced the Joe Paterno clan, and possibly the greatest college coach of all time.

The current Western definition of Byzantine is a pejorative and misnomer. Until Rome officially accepted Christianity as the state religion (500 years after Christ) all Christians used some intrigue to survive.

Our father, Angelo Lafayette Paterno, was the son of a Barber. He was one of six children: Victor, Rose, Francine, Marie, Angelo and Frederick, who all made their mark in their communities. Victor was a successful lawyer and real estate agent and Rose was a teacher and linguist. Francine was a politician whose son Joseph became President of Motorola (Canada); Marie was a painter and author; and our Uncle Fred, a writer, was one of the editors of the original *Brooklyn Eagle*, a true Renaissance man. And there was of course our father, Angelo, a legal clerk of the Supreme Court, and a lawyer. All of the Paternos were educated and intellectually idealistic, pro education and successful. They were compassionate and humanistic, but also very competitive.

Our mother's name was Florence DeLasalle Cafiero, one of ten children; seven sisters and three brothers. Her father, our grandfather, had red hair and owned a successful produce company long before Italians had influence in that market. Most of his friends were Irish. He had horses and carts, and he carried a bullwhip and a gun when he went to work. My mother and her clan lived in a three-story home on Troy Avenue in Brooklyn, New York. It was known as the house of laughter because of the seven sisters who lived there and the wine that flowed. One of the Cafiero offsprings became President of Chrysler. Eugene Cafiero, the son of the oldest brother, Anthony Cafiero, my cousin, Gene, rose through the ranks and preceded Lee Iaccoca as President. Less educated and less idealistic than the Paternos, the Cafieros were fiercely clannish, ferociously competitive, had great street smarts and animal instincts, and boy were they tough.

Politically, our father would be called a Rooseveltian Democrat and the Cafieros, quintessential Republicans. The Cafieros were Neopolitans and Sorrentese. All of the children were fair skinned, and the girls were considered attractive. My mother, Florence, had blonde hair as a young woman, and immense, piercing green eyes. We called her Ollie the Owl. She hardly slept, was fanatically clean, could be totally selfish, excessively demanding and was absolutely fearless. Her generosity flowed in accordance with her good fortune and when she knew she had more than others. My mother was obsessed at being the best. Her sisters did not marry as well, but my father shared any advantages we had. He did all of the legal work for the family gratis, and his brothers-in-law called him a "Prince." In some ways, my mother resented the educated Paternos and their free-thinking ways. She tried and was successful in exposing her children mainly to the Cafiero clan.

As I grew up, I resented her attitude and unfairness. Dad, for the sake of peace, rolled with the punches. By the way, no one called my father Angelo, he was called Pat. I am sure Mom felt it was a "wop" name and we had to prove ourselves superior to our neighbors, friends, and competitors. My mother lived to be 92. She outlived my father by 33 years and outlived all of her siblings. I think she died because she was bored. Joe Paterno is a clone of his mother, both mentally and physically, but he also inherited many of my Dad's best qualities, and they produced a superior hybrid offspring.

Joe Paterno was the first child produced by Angelo Paterno and Florence Cafiero. The Byzantine values blended with the Neapolitan (possibly a touch of Teutonic), earthiness and charm produced four children: Joe, George, Franklin, and a sister named Florence, whom we call Cissy. Franklin Paterno died of pneumonia as an infant.

From the time of his birth, Joe was always the top banana in our mother's eyes and would remain that way until she died. Her influence on him was so great she forgave his shortcomings and almost eulogized him; instilling great inner confidence, something the other children lacked. Probably that is why Joe married a woman much like his mother. Strong willed, family oriented, a second mother who allowed him to pursue his genetic instincts for greatness. For some reason, both families—the Paterno and Cafieros—intermarried mostly with Germans, Irish or Swedes. Certainly Joe did. His wife Sue is German by both parents.

When does a cognizant sibling relationship begin? I am sure psychologists would say it begins with some emotional incident, and so it was between Joe and me. When Joe was approximately 3 1/2 and I about 2 years old, I tried to take a small rake away from him, the kind of rake kids play with in the sand. He responded by hitting me in the face; leaving a scar on my nose that I still have. From that point on I knew he would not easily give up his possessions. As we grew up, our fights continued. The classic one occurred in front of a shoe store on Avenue U and Homecrest Avenue in Brooklyn, where we then resided. He was about 6 and I was about 4 1/2. I hit him with a bicycle chain that I had found. He took it from me and threw it at me. I ducked and it went through the large plate glass window of the store. Of course my Dad had to pay for the damage. We both ran like hell, but everyone knew where we lived. As I was hiding under the bed, my father, along with Joe, found me and I was punished. I think Joe got off for his honesty in reporting the incident. As usual, my mother felt that Joe could do no wrong.

As we got older, I felt that my Dad was beginning to favor me (maybe he thought I needed the attention). Mom didn't like that, but maybe it was because she thought Dad's family was giving me a little more attention than Joe. To be honest, I adored my father, but I did not like my mother, and of course I did not know what fate had planned for me.

From Homecrest Avenue we moved to 18th Street between Avenue U and Avenue T, one block from St. Edmund's parish. It was there we went to Catholic grammar school and made most of our friendships that have endured to present times. We lived across the street from an Italian family named Mastiloni, who were in the diamond and pearl business. They were good people and became highly successful. But they and the Spedutos were the only Italian families we knew. Almost all of our friends were of Irish decent; the Murnanes, the McKennas, the Reardons, the O'Haras, the Hundleys, the Bennetts, the Caldwells, the Reillys, and others. They came from outstanding middle-class families, family oriented, with the proper amount of religious influence. They indeed were much like us. We all got along famously and some of their sons became national figures.

When my father died, Mr. Murnane handled the funeral arrangements. Ed Murnane and Frank Mastiloni still must be considered two of Joe Paterno's closest friends. If ever there was a wholesome matrix for good people to raise a family, it was our part of Flatbush, Brooklyn. After our youngest brother, Franklin, died of pneumonia, we moved to 23rd Street between T and S. Still in St. Edmunds parish, we were able to keep our friends and we continued our schooling. While living at the 23rd Street residence, two new additions came to the family. My sister Florence was born, who as I said before we called Cissy, and we got a dog for her, named Buddy, who we had for 17 years.

As we began to approach adolescence, the Paterno children became intensely interested in sports. Everybody played stickball, association, kick the can, boxball, stoopball, Johnny on the pony and marbles in the streets. We played between parked cars with a lot of minor traffic coming down the street. We played endlessly; it was a glorious time. Relationships were cemented and small friendly groups began to come together, usually based on age.

During these competitions came my first realization of Joe's need to win, his need to be number one. It wasn't a game, it was almost a maniacal need to be first. He competed on a level beyond the game. It was a rage to win, almost as if his life depended on it, just like Mom's need to be the best. If he lost he could be a sore loser, a deficiency he learned to control and he overcame with maturity. He tried never to cheat. If it was a game that failed to titillate his competitive instincts, he became bored. He didn't like fishing or hunting on a pedestrian level. When some of the guys went to Sheepshead Bay, (a famous boating and fishing area), to catch snapper, which were baby blue fish, or go crabbing, he usually remained home and read or listened to music.

The more I realized his need to win, the less desire I had to compete against him. Even if I could have won, it was not that important to me, certainly not as it was to him. He affected many people in the same fashion, and it became more important to help Joe win. Probably all great leaders project that quality to their followers.

Joe always was excessively serious and focused, even as a young boy. His seriousness caused him to wear a frown, and we kidded him and called him Joe Joe, "the dogfaced boy." What we didn't realize was that the frown was a result of thinking out each experience he might be exposed to.

Joe's need to be number one applied not only to sports, but also to studies. He was the darling of all of his teachers, the Nuns at St. Edmunds, the Jesuits at Brooklyn Prep, and later the Professors at Brown. While I hated school, he loved it. While I was content to just get by, he always wanted to be tops in his class. The Jesuits especially loved his attitude. When most of his peers were silly and out looking for fun, his objectives were to be first in everything. My Dad was proud, but my mother took it for granted. For sure Joe would be the next Clarence Darrow or perhaps Judge Cardoza, or the great trial lawyer, Farrell. I am not sure what Dad thought about me, but my mother certainly didn't understand me. Even if I did not realize it, in some ways I was the antithesis of Joe; a free spirit.

# Chapter Two

# HIGH SCHOOL DAYS, THE QUEST BEGINS

While living at 23rd Street in Brooklyn, Japan bombed Pearl Harbor. A flash came over the radio while Joe and I were listening to a football game (the old Brooklyn Dodgers), on Sunday. To this day, I remember the look on my father's face as he tried to explain to my mother what happened. The U.S. would be at war.

Time passed quickly at 23rd Street; Joe was responsible to get me home from St. Edmund's—a job, as usual, that he took seriously. In school, we practiced air raid alarm drills and had blackouts at night. Dad became the head of the block's Air Raid Wardens. Most of the wardens were the fathers of our friends.

My Dad had natural leadership qualities; he liked the military. In his late teens he had joined the Cavalry and chased Pancho Villa in Mexico. He became an expert horseman and rose to the rank of Sergeant. Dad was still in the Army when World War I broke out. He went to Europe and the cavalry became the artillery, and Dad fought in the Argonne and Verdun campaigns. After the war, he stayed in the National Guard and became a Captain. So it was natural for him to take charge of the Air Raid Wardens. As Joe's career started to take flight toward his present lofty position, too often he forgets to mention Dad. As I said, he was Mom's boy.

We were still living on 23rd Street when Joe became of high school age. He took tests for public high schools, Brooklyn Tech and others, and a Catholic High School, St. Augustine. He won free scholarships to both schools, but the best high school in the area was Brooklyn Prep, a Jesuit school. There was a tuition fee, though, that would have been a financial burden on my father. Brooklyn Prep was the best, and Joe had to have the best, so Mom intervened, and of course she prevailed. At Brooklyn Prep, students had to wear a coat and tie and have their own lunch, or money to purchase it. The Jesuits, since the counter reformation, always strived to outdo their rivals, the Parochial Protestant schools.

One must be honest though, the Jesuits had some of the best teachers and facilities. Many of their rank came from wealthy aristocratic families. They were sophisticated, could be extremely charming, and sometimes practiced sophistry. All of the above made them the priests for the upper middle class and higher. Financially, we didn't belong.

As a freshman, Joe immediately impressed all of the Jesuits with his intelligence, ambition and desire to be outstanding in studies. One particular Jesuit, Brother Tom Birmingham, was the first to realize this serious young boy was special. Later Brother Birmingham himself became famous as the advisor to William Peter Blatty, the author of the famous novel, *The Exorcist*. I too came under the spell of this Irish mystic, but for different reasons. Brother Birmingham would spend many hours after school personally tutoring Joe and translating Latin (especially *The Aeneid*). Certainly Joe had the proper blood line and the potential skills and pragmatic idealism to go to Rome. But that was not to be. To date, Brother Tom continues to be Joe's favorite priest and friend. Later, I will explain how Joe's bout with moralism almost ended the relationship.

In his freshman year at Brooklyn Prep, Joe went out for football but didn't make the team. He was a funny looking kid, a 135-lb. boy with half-inch pipes for legs. Would you believe that he went out for a guard position on the offensive line? The newly hired coach, (a former All-American from Fordham University and prior coach of Fordham Prep), a rival Jesuit school, cut Joe. Later, it was Coach Earl Graham who made the dramatic move that could have been the key to Joe Paterno's present career.

By the time Joe was going into his second year at Brooklyn Prep, I was ready for high school. What about George? I also got into St. Augustine, but they had no football team. A free ride, but certainly not Brooklyn Prep. I too wanted to go to Brooklyn Prep and play football, but my father was financially strapped paying for Joe's tuition, so he said no to my wishes. My Mother, for the first time, seemed to care, I guess because she thought I needed Joe to watch over me. I asked Dad to please let me go. My Father generally kept his financial problems from the family, but he said he didn't know if he could afford it. I promised him that if he let me attend Brooklyn Prep, I would win a football scholarship to college. Playing in the streets against bigger kids made me confident of my ability.

Angelo "Pat" Paterno, was determined to provide the best for his kids. He arranged for a visit with the Head Master of Brooklyn Prep, a Father Hooper. He told the good Jesuit of his problem. He wanted both sons to go to Prep but couldn't afford the tuition. Father Hooper arranged for both of us to attend school for a tuition and one half. Joe's outstanding impression probably had some influence on the priest's decision. So when I was fourteen, I too was admitted to Brooklyn Prep.

Going into a second year at Brooklyn Prep, the course had been set, the frown became deeper, the goals more apparent, the methodology more formalized and the sibling relationship more individualistic. Because of Dad's love and Father Hooper's generosity, both of the Paterno boys attended Brooklyn Prep at the same time for three years. My mother had her way; I am not sure it was good for me.

A year prior to my going to the Prep, I was transforming from a child into an adolescent; my features were changing, and my nose began to grow. I wasn't the Elephant Man, and probably didn't look much different than Joe, but Mom made an issue out of it. She used to tell me when I went to bed to put a sock on my nose with stones and throw it over my head so my nose would grow up and not down. She made jokes for the benefit of her sisters. I felt I wasn't going to be presentable to other people. By the time I got to high school, I thought I was a combination of Pinocchio and Cyrano De Bergerac. It was then I concluded that I would accept myself come hell or high water. Physical danger became appealing and inconsequential and later led me to take a cavalier attitude toward life or death. Fellow students are at a cruel age early in high school and they compounded the problem by making fun of me. Little did I know that there was nothing really wrong with me; I was just going through growing pains.

When I entered Brooklyn Prep, Joe was a sophomore. Even as a 16-year-old sophomore, the Byzantine personality was becoming formalized and shaped. The Jesuit influence was the perfect catalyst to hone his innate strengths and temper the explosive personality with calculating, patience, and manipulative skills. As a high school sophomore, he was one of the leaders of his class, getting superior grades and planning his future. He was a Class Beadle, (an attendance reporter), and a personal representative of Father Frank Brock, the Athletic Director and Prefect of Discipline. In addition to reporting absenteeism in his own class, he collected absentee slips for the entire school. His first step on the ladder was taken. My days of playing hookie were over, eventually he had to report me, what else was new? Of course he was doing the right thing.

As a sophomore, once again Joe went out for football. This time he made the squad as a substitute guard. Joe was probably 5'10", 140 lbs., skinny legs, and a brainy member of a very mediocre high school football team. Although he didn't play much, Dad and I went to every game. Joe's big moment as a sophomore was in a Mount St. Michael game, a powerful team. Brooklyn Prep lost, but Joe recovered the kick off (free ball) for a touchdown. The rest of the team didn't know the rules. The seed was planted—Coach Graham had plans for this bright kid for the future.

As Joe was going into his junior year and I into my sophomore year, I had impressed some of the older boys with my skills in the school yard, so I again went out for the football team. This time we both made the first team; I was a running back, and Joe was the new quarterback. Coach Earl Zev-Graham converted the smart, tough, skinny kid to a quarterback. The launching pad had been fueled for both of us.

At the same time, my father made sacrifices to pay for our education, he had passed the Bar. It was a great achievement; Pat Paterno had gone to St. John's Law School at night, while working full time and raising a family. He used to fall asleep in his chair studying after dinner. I will never forget during one winter blizzard he sat in his chair  in our home without heat with his overcoat and hat on studying to get his law degree for the benefit of his family. He actually fell asleep, fully clothed with his law book in hand; he went to work the next morning.

Dinner at our house was always fun. Dad encouraged discussion on all topics, current and past, and about our school work. Arguments were the norm. Mom's role was cooking and serving a hearty meal; these were some of the few occasions when she didn't vocally participate. Our sister was beginning to grow into a beautiful girl. Eventually Mom started the nose bit on Cis, and she too had an inferiority complex, but as she grew up to be an extremely good looking female, it passed. Many years later when I was left alone with Mom, I realized that some of her actions that had seemed cruel at the time were not based on malice, but were because of ignorance of what damage she might have been doing.  Mostly, she was driven by the need to be better than everyone and that most certainly included her family. We used to joke about her making us wear a shirt and sometimes a tie just to put out the garbage.

One day at school, I inadvertently bumped into an upper classman, the son of a judge who was of Irish nationality. He cursed me, and for the first time I was called a Guinea. Naturally, I knew it was a slur and instinctively struck him. From that point on, I got a reputation for being a roughneck, a title I didn't like.

You see, at home, we never heard a curse word or a disparaging remark about any race, religion or ethnic group, and our Irish friends from St. Edmunds never used such insults. But Brooklyn Prep was not St. Edmunds. Most of the students at Brooklyn Prep came from money and some were what middle-class Irish would describe as "lace curtain Irish". There were also some students from wealthy Italian families, usually doctors or contractors.

In a short time, Joe would win them over and become president of the student council. He had the student body, as well as the Jesuits, eating out of his hand. The only goal Joe failed to accomplish at Brooklyn Prep was being voted captain of the football team in his senior year. Two of his best buddies, Joe Murphy and Bill Snyder became co-captains, but everyone knew Joe was the leader of his team.

Playing as a senior, Joe became the brainy quarterback. Dick Reilly, Charles Weiss and I were the running backs. It was an outstanding squad, some say the best ever of our high school. However, we did lose one game. Across the river in Englewood, New Jersey, was a school called St. Cecelia's. They had won 47 straight games, and the coach's name was Vince Lombardi. A portent of the future? It was a close game. Joe, Bill Snyder and Joe Murphy all had been hurt the week before playing against the strong Mount St. Michael's team, another perennial high school power. Joe took a "shot" in the shoulder to kill the pain because he  also played defensive linebacker and would be hit often. Star offensive linemen Murphy and Snyder were also injured. I had a big day, but we lost. Little did we know the greatness of the team and the coach we lost to.  In those days players went both ways, with no face masks or mouth guards. Later Lombardi went on to coach at Fordham University, the New York Giants, the Green Bay Packers, and became a legend. As we shall see, Joe Paterno went to Brown and Penn State to build his own legend. Two guys from the same mold, two clones, who in their respective ways on different levels would not only change the record books, but the image of football forever.

Because of the outstanding record in '44, Joe was voted All-Metropolitan, a most distinguished achievement. He also was president of the student body and one of the top students in the school.

The war was coming to an end, fascism was being defeated around the world. Catholicism from Rome was becoming more liberal. Pope Pius was replaced by John. Christianity was solidifying to battle the threat of world-wide Communism. Ecumenicism was being established; the Catholics and the Protestants were reuniting under the realm of true Christianity. The animosity between the Parochial Protestant colleges, (Ivy League especially), and the Parochial Catholic Schools, the Jesuits, Notre Dame was ameliorating.

# Chapter Three

# BROWN UNIVERSITY

One day a man came to our house whose name was George Bennett. He represented Everett "Busy" Arnold, a comic book mogul. Mr. Bennett told my Dad that he was entrusted by Mr. Arnold to help build the football program at Brown University, a most prestigious academic school that had suffered bad days in football. In those days, like all schools, the Ivy League gave full scholarships. Joe was offered a full scholarship to Brown University. The next step in Joe's trek to greatness had been taken. But he had to wait until he finished his service time to attend Brown. In that interim, I also accepted a scholarship to Brown.

Joe got off to a bad start at Brown. While waiting for the train to go to Providence at Grand Central Station, he called home to reassure Mom that he was okay. During his conversation in the booth, all of his luggage was stolen and Joe Paterno started college, literally, with only the clothes on his back. Having been accepted prior to going into the service, as a veteran he was eligible to play varsity football, and so he reported early. I, not being a veteran, was ineligible for the varsity and reported two weeks later for indoctrination.

Also deciding to go to Brown under the Arnold Foundation was Joe's best buddy, Joe Murphy, another outstanding Brooklyn Prep athlete. Bucky Walters and Frank Mahoney's brother, Walter, also attended, as did friends Bob Shaughnessy and Harry Scanlon. Joe Murphy left after his first year to enter the Seminary. Murphy eventually left the secular seminary, and became prominent in the CIA. Walter Mahoney, Shaughnessy and Scanlon tried football but gave it up. They were veterans and wanted to concentrate on their studies. They didn't make the varsity, but Mr. Arnold continued to provide legal financial assistance.

When the Paterno brothers, Frank Mahoney and Bucky Walters became stalwarts on possibly the best team in Brown's history, in 1949, they also beat Holy Cross (a Jesuit college). The Brooklyn Prep Jesuits suddenly had doubts about the new ecumenical approach to  letting their students go to a non-Catholic school.

One of the reasons many of the Catholic Jesuit students went to a  Protestant school like Brown was that their fathers were worldly and had faith in their kids.  It was also due to the presence of Brown's coach Charles (Rip) Engle, a kindly, religious, handsome gray-haired gentleman who was a father figure himself. Rip Engle would have a tremendous impact on Joe's career in many ways, and his influence on Joe is revealed in Joe's later life.

There were not too many Italian students at Brown, but there were former players like Gammino, Saviano and Bonnana. In fact Brown, playing in the first Rose Bowl, had the first black player in the Ivy League, Fritz Pollard, an All-American. Originally, all of the schools that were called the "Ivy League" began as Parochial Sectarian Theology schools. Later the league was formed and called the Ivy League.

The Paternos sure were stepping up in the social world. At Brooklyn Prep we were exposed to  wealthy members of the neighborhood. At Brown, we rubbed elbows and became friends with some of the richest and most aristocratic families in the country. I would need a whole chapter to mention the famous families we got to know. Various anecdotes in this book will allude to the many interesting people we became familiar with.

Joe's initial experience as a football player was quite in-auspicious. He was recruited as a quarterback, didn't look very ominous, and had several older established quarterbacks ahead of him. There was Hank Pilot, Paul Gaffney and Pres Barry, all good players—not great players—but more importantly, beautiful human beings.

So Joe didn't play as a freshman, but Rip Engle saw some athletic skills in this bright, wiry kid from Brooklyn and so he made him a defensive back. By the end of his playing career, Joe probably was remembered more for his defensive skills than his quarterback achievements. I think he still has the record for interceptions.

Once again, his great feel for the game got him in the right place at the right time to make big plays. The year was 1947, and by the end of Joe's first year at Brown, he had established himself as an outstanding student, a potential quarterback, and a candidate for a fraternity. The DKE, known primarily as a jock fraternity, also had the dubious reputation as the drunken dekes. What a crew!!

The year is 1946. The war being over, veterans had served many years in the Armed Forces. The incoming freshman class age ranged from 18 to 27. There were students who had five years in the service and previously had been in prep school. Many of the vets were entitled to schooling under the GI Bill of Rights and now could afford to go to a prestigious Ivy League school. For years, the Ivy universities catered to the rich and aristocratic and were very proud of their legacy enrollment from venerable families. But now, those who were academically eligible could get government funding for the school of their choice. The result was a representation that was the greatest melange of people from diversified backgrounds that ever entered the university. There were the rich, middle class of all levels, and the poor; every ethnic, religious and racial group was represented.

This was especially true with the football team. The varied mixture was  the catalystic chemistry that produced the success of the '48 and '49 teams, and Coach Engle was the perfect maestro.

Brown had then an infrastructure of romance that it never had before and maybe will never have again. As soon as it was feasible, the school's administration raised tuition rates out of the reach of the GI candidates, (all of the Ivy League schools followed suit). They wanted to return to the prewar days of educating the elite and the avant grade and collecting large future endowments. But for a span of six years, the Waspish upper class with families from IBM, Standard Oil, and U.S. Steel, and had to rub elbows with the Paterno brothers, the Walters and Mahoneys from Brooklyn, and people like Fred Kozack, Don Colo, (future captain of the famous Cleveland Browns), Ed Kiley, all from the Foundries and the blue collar families of New England.

With Rip Engle as his mentor, Joe Paterno became the leader of this diverse group. Joe and the team center, John Scott, who eventually became CEO of the Vicks Corporation, were co-captains. This time Joe did not let the captaincy elude him. I was the youngest member of the team at 18, and Joe Condon, our field goal and extra point kicker, was the oldest member at 27.

Before reporting to Brown in 1946, I had thought about going into the Jesuit Order. Although I had a successful senior year playing football at Brooklyn Prep, I had gone more and more into a shell, completely lacking social confidence. My consideration of a vocation was a form of escape. No matter what I looked like, I felt I could do a great deal of good in the priesthood. This was the persona I brought to Brown University in 1946, being a kid among older players who were veterans, many of whom had seen a great deal of combat. They were tough, mature and just happy to be alive. They were great guys, but they too would have fun at my expense. As Joe grew more and more outgoing and confident, I was losing confidence and my inferiority complex was evident in a cavalier attitude toward everything. Going into the midst of these worldly veterans was a guy, who outside of his senior prom, never had a date and didn't drink or smoke.

Many people have asked me what I learned from my older veteran teammates, and my reply was they taught me how to drink, curse, and be aware of women. By the end of our first and second years, Joe was the Man for all Seasons, a great student, excellent athlete and a popular leader among the team and his fraternity brothers. Although I did okay in football and got along, my greatest accomplishment was to be the best pinochle player in my dorm. A dubious distinction, but I managed to survive academically. I chose Economics as my major, a subject I knew little about and for which I had even less aptitude. My first preference would have been art. As a child I loved to draw and appreciate art, but art majors were mostly women, and I was uncomfortable with and almost afraid of females.

Once again, Joe was focused on what he wanted and I was going in the opposite direction. Joe was the pragmatic brother, but I started to realize that I was becoming a free spirit, a feeling that had been shackled by my mother's influences and by my own complexes.

# Chapter Four

# THE TEAM

The football team at Brown in 1948 won seven games and the cry was "9 for 9 in '49." Between '46 and '48, the chaff was separated from the wheat. What remained was a corps of hard-nosed, skilled players. We were two deep in every position. Joe and I both played some offense and some defense. Joe shared quarterback duties with Ed Finn, a better passer, and a local high school star. The players liked Joe better and he was in the game when we wanted to run the ball. Finn was a cocky, self-centered guy, who I felt resented the Brooklyn players. Remember, this was 1948.

Joe was improving as a passer, and to increase his throwing ability he spent the entire summer vacation throwing a medicine ball against the cellar wall. It paid dividends. I shared fullback duties with a tough Jewish kid named Arnie Green. Arnie was a bit like Joe, he overcame a lack of natural skills with desire and toughness. He also was Ed Finn's buddy and fraternity brother from Sigma Chi. I seldom touched the ball when Finn was quarterback. Understanding the situation, it didn't bother me too much as I got my share of playing time, but it made me determined to win the fullback job the following season.

Outside of that minor situation, there were few cliques and no politics among the players; this was truly a team. The politics that surfaced were due to the competition of the alumni who made the largest donations to the football program, namely, our sponsor, Busy Arnold from New York, and Daddy Fales, the big contributor from Rhode Island. Mr. Fales came to all of our practices with his personal chair and watched his boys. He was a nice man, but he liked to feel that his efforts were rewarded by seeing his players do well. Busy Arnold only came to see some games. He was making a ton of money and had a penthouse in Manhattan, a place in Naples, Florida, as well as a home in Scarsdale, NY. However, it seemed that more of Busy's boys were doing better than Fales'.

For the first time I became aware that Rip was playing some politics. After all, he wanted to maintain the support of his chief benefactors. Example: In one backfield, Arnold was the sponsor of Joe, me, Chuck Nelson from Brooklyn and Roger Young from Long Island. The other unit had Ed Finn, Fred Kozac, Arnie Green and Marty Gresh, all sponsored By Fales from New England. We all played, but it was a trade off. As a young idealist and the youngest on the team, I became a bit disenchanted. Although I admired and respected Green, I felt that I was better and could have really contributed a great deal more. Maybe it was my youth, but I didn't really play up to some of my capabilities. I had some good games, but I was inconsistent. Although Joe was a better runner and smarter than Finn, he got less playing time. However, he was a first-string defensive back. I only played sparingly on defense. Things would be different in '49.

Joe handled the competition with maturity and confidence in the future. He learned playing a little politics was part of the coaches' right to produce the desired outcome. When Joe became Rip's assistant, he would learn a great deal more about how to handle people in a football program. Conforming was not my forte.

Once in a discussion about abstract values of right and wrong, Joe said that I had better learn to bend a bit to get along and be successful. All he was doing was proffering what many religious orders have promulgated through the years. It is okay if it is for the "greater good", and one stays within the parameters of morality. But when does the philosophy become rationalization and a segue into hypocrisy? It is still difficult for me to accept the "greater good" hypothesis, if the action is contradictory to an absolute concept of morality. If morality can be flexible to change relative to different societies, situations and times, it cannot be absolute and therefore it doesn't really exist. Do the mores of society establish the rules for success or failure, if the mores are set by the ruling few?

The year 1948 could have been the matrix for a team and many individual members of that organization. After going through a human blender of competition that weeded out athletic and personality imperfections, the remaining result was a force that would make its mark in the Ivy League and in Brown history.

Rip Engle knew he was about to make a significant move for our team in 1948. He had the support of the Brown Athletic Director, Paul Mackesey, former player, outstanding gentleman, and a big supporter of a wholesome football program. Rip had hired a great staff led by Weeb Ewbank as backfield coach, (later to be winner of two NFL Championships, for two different teams; and an NFL Hall of Famer). The line coach was Gus Zitrides, one of the original watchcharm guards from Dartmouth, later to be Personnel Representative for the CIA.

Joe McMullen was another line coach, later to be the Athletic Director at Marshall University, and Papa Dunne, former pro coach of Canada, and other outstanding people like Bob Priestly, Ernie Saviano, Pat O'Brien and Ernie Solloway. The team doctor was Ed Crane, a local man who loved every player as part of his family. The last and most famous was trainer Jack McKinnen, the curmudgeon genius with tape, linament and counsel. We were ready.

In 1948 we won seven games, beating Ivy League teams who graduated players who became outstanding professionals in the NFL. We beat a Princeton team with three All-Americans and future Heisman winner, Dick Kazmaier. That Princeton team went on to win 17 in a row.

Most important, personalities were now being developed. The anonymous group who enrolled in 1946 had overcome their postwar problems and had become part of a legacy. The confused, amorphous melange had become a formidable uniform group with the same goals molded together with perfect chemistry. Rip Engle, who majored in chemistry, had found the correct formula. Joe Paterno became the Bunsen Burner that heated the chemical ingredients.

The spring practice prior to the '49 season was intense, (in those days Ivy League schools not only tendered scholarships, but had a month of spring practice drills). Everyone smelled a big year, and Joe finally had the quarterback job all to himself. His backup would be a big Polish fellow with the fine name of Walt Pastusak; he had a strong arm but lacked Joe's experience. Walter later became a fine quarterback, a high school coach, and a dear friend.

This was going to be Joe's team and he seized the moment. He and John Scott were voted co-captains, probably the two brightest guys on the team. With three years of experience, Joe was like a coach on the field; he knew everyone's assignment on every play and he studied defenses as intently as he studied his school subjects. Most players only worry about their respective assignments, hoping not to make any mistakes.

During the first week of spring practice, I suffered a severe rib cartilage injury and was sidelined for the remaining time. Naturally, I became depressed thinking my chances to be the sole starter in '49 were gone. But poor Arnie Green suffered a career-ending knee injury in the fall and the job was mine.

Going into that '49 season I had read *The Razor's Edge* by Somerset Maugham. I began to fantasize that I was "Larry", the main character in the book who went off in search of the truth and became a bit of a mystic. That would be my role in life. Eventually I attempted to put my fantasy into practice and traveled extensively but not to the Far East. In 1949, Joe Paterno began his journey to be a living legend. Newspaper writers admired his leadership and wit. We were winning impressively and he played both ways when most people, including me, were singularly platooned. Stanley Woodward, the great sportswriter, said, "Joe Paterno couldn't pass or run, all he could do was think and win". Actually, Joe could run; he had deceptive speed and his passing was adequate. He made some quarterback keeper runs that beat Harvard and many of his interceptions turned the tide in big games.

A columnist for the *Providence Journal* named John Hanlon (also a war veteran), loved the team and especially loved Joe. We stumbled once and lost to a great Princeton team that went on to win 17 straight and produced many All-Americans. A couple of breakdowns in the secondary allowed Kazmaier to complete two easy touchdown passes and we lost a close game. Joe's shadow became larger and larger.

I too had a good season; I was the leading ground gainer, averaging around five yards per carry and scored eight TDs. But some people hardly knew I played. One frustrating write-up had Joe throwing himself a pass (naturally it was to me).

As the years passed, the Paterno brothers became Joe Paterno. I admired him, so it didn't bother me. By the time we graduated, I knew where he was going, but I was not so sure about myself. Our philosophies began to drift apart. We were both idealists. I was the intransigent romantic and Joe tempered his idealism with practicality.

# Chapter Five

# PENN STATE

The combined record of '48 and '49 made Rip Engle a hot item as a coach. Rip's background prior to getting the Brown job was at a high school in Pennsylvania, and as an assistant at Western Maryland under his former college coach Dick Harlow, who had also been a coach at Penn State. Harlow became a coach at Colgate but was really known for his outstanding success at Harvard. When we finally beat Harvard, it was a great win for Rip over his old mentor. Rip was a natural to be selected as the new coach at Penn State. After Bob Higgins, a great coach himself, Penn State had an interim coach, Joe Bedenk, the man Rip replaced.

Rip Engle, although always successful, was an underrated coach, mostly because of his Quaker values, placidity and humility. Actually, he was exceedingly intense and imaginative. His interpretation of offense was called a side-saddle T formation. This was a mix of what is called a wing T, but with the quarterback set behind the center's butt, offset to one side. He also was one of the first coaches to use motion away from and toward the formation while maintaining power blocking schemes of the popular single wing. Actually, it was a complex system, so when taking on a new job, it would help to have a backfield coach who knew the operation. Who better to be his first new assistant than his intense, bright quarterback who helped him win 15 games in two years, a record at Brown. Joe Paterno was the choice.

Rip's offer caught Joe by surprise. To appease my Dad, Joe had taken the Legal Boards at Princeton and to no one's surprise, he finished in the top 10 percent nationally. Dad was so excited because he was about to retire and planned to build a house on Long Island and open up his own law office. Wouldn't it be great to have a son as a partner? Joe had a big decision to make. He loved football. It was an extension of his personality and he liked the attention. He also wanted to please Dad, and I am sure he foresaw a potential great legal career. What to do? Pragmatic Joe had a solution; he wanted to try coaching for one year and if he didn't like it, he would go to law school. The year was 1950. As we all know now, Joe is still at Penn State so I guess he made the right decision, but Dad made it easy. I was there when he said to Joe, "Do what you feel is in your best interest", so Joe went off to Penn State with a peaceful mind.

When Rip took over, he brought Joe and Joe McMullen, the line coach from Brown, but he kept most of the prior staff at Penn State: Jim O'Hora, Sever Toretti, Frank Patrick and Earl Bruce—the freshman coach, also Earl Edwards. All were excellent coaches and teachers and future friends and advisors to my brother.

Joe arrived at Penn State alone, ambitious, volatile and anxious to show everyone how smart he was. Rip Engle ran a professional, low-key coaching staff. Weeb Ewbank had left Brown in 1948 to go with the Cleveland Browns and the great coach Paul Brown. Rip needed a strong right hand and he had enough confidence in this young Brooklyn kid, who some said looked like an Italian Saxophone player.

Early on, Joe irritated his fellow coaches with his emotional and aggressive style. Even some of the players made fun of his pipe-like legs. After all, he was only slightly older than the players, being 22. This was exactly the exposure this brash individual needed.

It was then that Joe met a former Penn State All-American and a former All-Pro with the Pittsburgh Steelers, Steve Suhey. Steve had retired from professional football and had married coach Bob Higgins' daughter, Virginia, who everyone calls Ginger. After being married, Steve and Ginger settled in Bellefonte and would later come back and live in State College, (Happy Valley). Steve couldn't stay away from football and began to help out on a volunteer basis. He and Joe became great friends; he invited Joe to rent a room in his house, and Joe accepted.

Steve, Joe, Ginger and her friend, June, who eventually married one of Steve's Penn State teammates, Bob Hicks, all became fast friends. It was good for Joe being with such nice people. I always felt that they helped Joe make his decision to stay at Penn State. If there are better people in the world, I challenge anyone to find them.

Although Ginger's aunt was a nationally known figure, Margaret Sanger, an advocate for birth control, she and Steve immediately started to have a family and eventually had seven children. The children began to come right away, so Joe had to find new dwellings. Joe wanted to stay there, but there just wasn't enough room. Steve gave him ample time to find another place and Joe moved to the O'Hora residence. Joe can't handle being alone; he has to be around people (something I learned to overcome as a bachelor).

A few years later, after our father died, Steve and Ginger would always invite me and my Mom to dinner at their house at Bellefonte. In those years I used to drive Mom up to see Joe on Route 22, sometimes in severe winter weather. We would see Joe and the Suheys. Their supper table was right out of Americana; Ginger, Steve, the kids, guests, Mom and me, sometimes with Joe, and of course the chicken, the mashed potatoes, and vegetables, but most of all, excessive kindness. Eventually, when Joe became head coach, he benefited from the Suhey family. Three of the Suhey boys played for Penn State, Matt, Steve and Paul. I became attached to Steve Suhey, senior; he was an outstanding man and helped Joe become

part of the Penn State community. The Suheys were an extension of the Paterno family. I hope Joe never forgets their kindness.

After returning from the service in 1953, I became one
of New York's finest. Once again Joe benefitted from the kindness of strangers. Defensive line coach Jim O'Hora and his
wife, Betts, who had three children, had rented Joe a room. Of
all the fine people Joe was fortunate to meet, I think Jim O'Hora
had the most dramatic and positive influence on him.

O'Hora was an outstanding coach himself, and Joe and
he would do battle for hours sitting at the kitchen bar dis-
cussing the strategies and techniques of football. Poor Betts,
she had to listen while trying to raise her family. Joe and Jim's
personalities were opposites; Joe the emotional shouter, Jim
the placid, quiet one. The O'Horas were the personification
of the best of the Irish breed. Joe learned he could get things
accomplished without shouting people down. Moreover, he
was given access to a warm family atmosphere that he cher-
ished and needed. Some people said Joe was Jim's adopted
older son. The O'Horas are alive and well with their children
and grandchildren and still live in State College.

After seven years, Jim finally threw Joe out and told him
to get married and have a family of his own. Jim was like our
own father. Eventually Jim and Sever Toretti, (the charismatic
offensive line coach), stepped aside and allowed Joe a clear
shot at replacing Rip Engle in 1966. O'Hora remained as the
defensive coordinator and Toretti as the offensive line coach
helping Joe to take Penn State to the next level. The other
assistant coaches, Frank Patrick, Earl Bruce, and J.T. White
also remained loyal. As the years rolled by, many new outstanding men would be added to the staff. Men like George
Welsh, Jerry Sandusky, Fran Ganter, Dick Andersen, John
Chuckran, all outstanding coaches and fine people. Joe too
was developing as a coach and getting ready for the Penn
State-Army game, when our father suddenly died from a heart
attack.

My father, who was contemplating retirement when
reaching his 30th year of civil service employment took a

ride with me, Mom and my Aunt Mary, to see how the new house he was building in Wantaugh, Long Island, was progressing. I had returned from my stint in the military service. After graduating from Brown I was called into the Marine Corps because of the Korean War. I was called in because in my junior year at Brown I enrolled in the Marine Platoon Leader program to become a Second Lieutenant. It was to be for two summers; six weeks each summer. Losing so much weight during the first session, (17 pounds!), I reported for fall practice tired and underweight and dropped out of the program.

Although I left the Platoon Leader program, I didn't realize I was still in the Reserves as a Corporal, so much to my surprise I was called into the service after graduation. Consequently, I had a right to a veteran's mortgage with low interest rates, so Dad used that to purchase the new house he was never to see. At that time, we were living at East 29th Street. We all were at home one day; Cissy was also back from school, and we sat down and had a nice dinner, and my Aunt was still there. After dinner Dad was helping Mom and my Aunt clean up. Cissy was upstairs and I was on the couch. Dad never said a word but he went to a chair and sat down in distress. Our family doctor, Dr. Kelly, was not available so I called the Civil Service Hospital Insurance Plan (HIP) Doctor. He came, put a stethoscope on Dad's heart and said, "How long have you had this condition?"

Dad just smiled. He had been working very hard. Cissy was to be married to a local boy, Warren Quaid, in six weeks, and he was hustling around to make some money to pay for a tony wedding at the Fifth Avenue Hotel in New York City. If Joe was the apple of Mom's eye, Cissy was Dad's joy, and so it should be.

As the Doctor removed the stethoscope, Dad fell forward. I caught him before he hit the floor. By the time I caught him in my arms he was dead. All hell broke loose. I was alone with Mom, Aunt Mary, and my 18-year-old sister. While I was comforting my Mother, the Doctor sneaked out and left me alone with the body. Later he explained to the police that Dad was not his patient and didn't want to sign the Death Certificate, but the police forced him to do so by law.

As I said, at that time I was a member of the New York City Police Department, and maybe that helped. I was going to fight crime and help improve the world. My sister showed exceptional courage and maturity during the entire sorrowful experience.

When I called for Joe he was still living at the O'Hora's. Jim O'Hora received my call; Joe was not at home. Jim tried to comfort me and said he would go out and look for Joe. Joe later called to say he was on the way home. When he arrived, he broke down in front of Mom. That time and when his son David almost died were the only times I have ever seen my brother Joe cry. For some reason I didn't shed a tear. Maybe because I saw it coming. Dad was just trying to do too much.

Six weeks later we had a beautiful wedding ceremony for my sister and Warren Quaid, with a great reception at the Number One Fifth Avenue Hotel. After my father's death, Joe had to go back to work, only to return for Cissy's wedding. I cleaned out Dad's locker and took care of all the paperwork. Mom was left a meager Life Insurance Policy and a small pension. Dad also had left some debts he had accumulated.

Through the years it has been written that Joe took care of everything following my father's death, and that is not true. He doesn't even know that my entire service allotment checks were sent home to Dad so he could pay for our sister to go to Marymount College, a super prestigious girl's college for the wealthy. I guess it was there that Cissy, rubbing elbows and making friends with the well to do, assumed we were financially well off. At that time, Joe knew very little about the family problems, he was away pursuing his career. Of course there was nothing wrong with that, it was just his destiny. The cards dealt to me were my fate and I intended to play them as best I could.

After Dad's death I found out about the true nature of some people. Dad's sister Marie, my Uncle Fred, and Dad's mother and father had preceded him in death. Only my Uncle Victor and my Aunt Rose and Frances were left from the Paternos. A month after Dad's death, my Uncle Victor called and reminded me that Dad owed him $500.00. I paid him immediately but I lost respect for him. He was always the distant brother. Dad was close to my sweet Uncle Fred. Maybe Uncle Victor's wife, Ruth Bacon, of English heritage, kept him from being close to our family. Possibly the dominating Cafiero sisters were too much for her and maybe she was right. But families should take priority, even over a railing wife. Too many men take the easy way out. In-law problems are universal and shouldn't be the cause of splitting sibling relations like my Uncle Victor and Dad.

# Chapter Six

# JOE RECRUITS A WIFE

fter leaving the O'Horas, Joe finally rented his own place and set out to follow O'Hora's advice to get married and have a family. Until he finally did get married, he was seldom in the small duplex he rented. He was so busy recruiting, visiting and speaking in clinics, with spring practice and then with the season itself, I am surprised he had time to find the future Mrs. Paterno. His big social hangout was the Elks or the American Legion, where he would have a few beers.

One day, Joe, an English major, was smitten by a young coed approaching graduation. Her name was Sue Pohland. She was buxom, had hair much like Mom's, was attractive and very intelligent. She also was an English major, but she was a coed, and in those days faculty members didn't dare date students. Cupid found a way, and although Joe was 13 years older, Sue found him attractive. When she graduated and took a summer job in Avon, New Jersey, Joe rented a cottage for the summer in Belmar, New Jersey. In those days, Assistant Coach's salaries were meager, but Joe was always prudent with his money and with Rip's advice had made some good investments. When he told me about the summer rental, I knew this was serious. Sue was a waitress and lived at the restaurant but she and Joe saw each other every day. When she worked, he worked, and on her days off he took off, and the romance blossomed.

Two weeks into the summer, Joe called me and asked me to bring Mom down to Belmar to meet Sue. For sure this was serious, but I didn't know how to tell Mom. After explaining that Joe, at the age of 34, was courting a girl, my Mom's big green eyes showed her concern. Suddenly, I was hit with a barrage of questions that I couldn't answer. I had never met my future sister-in-law. So, one day on a prearranged date, early in the morning, I packed Mom in the car and went off to have lunch with Joe and Sue.

At about the same time, I was dating a beautiful girl named Mary Ellen Stewart, who was one of 11 children, all of them drop-dead good looking. The *New York Daily News* had put the family on the cover of their magazine section. Mr. Stewart had left his wife to raise the kids by herself, so they became extremely close. As handsome as they were, they suffered the inevitable hangups. Mary Ellen had cracked the shell of inferiority that I had built around myself. Although Mom liked Mary Ellen, she always put her family down. We almost married, but it wasn't to be. So I knew Sue was in for a tough meeting.

During the time between Dad's death and Joe's decision to marry in 1964, he had gained an outstanding reputation as one of the top assistant coaches in the country. His friends were future famous coaches, Darryl Royal (eventually of Texas), Vince Dooley, (Georgia), Tom Osborne, (present coach of Nebraska), and Bobby Bowden, (West Virginia and Florida State). Legendary coaches such as Woody Hayes, and Ben Schwartzwalder, as well as Rip Engle singled Joe out as a future great. Joe had other offers before getting the job at Penn State in 1966. Weeb Ewbank had risen from an assistant coach at Cleveland and at Brown, to a head Pro Coach for the eventual world champions, the Baltimore Colts. Weeb offered Joe an assistant's job. Joe said no and Weeb hired Don Shula, who retired as the winningest coach in the history of pro football. Yale was also interested in hiring Joe. After all, he had an Ivy League background and was part of a big-time successful program. Prestigious Yale got Joe's attention; he wanted to stay at Penn State and replace Rip when he retired, but that was a tremendous gamble.

Ernie McCoy was the Athletic Director at Penn State. Ernie was a graduate of Michigan where he played football. He was a handsome, tall man, ramrod straight with a strong handshake. Ernie told Joe he wanted him to stay at Penn State and promised him that when Rip retired, if he was still Athletic Director, Joe would get the job. Joe grasped Ernie's strong hand and they shook on the agreement. Joe stayed, and Ernie, true to his word, appointed him head coach in 1966.

However, the climb was not easy. Besides the endless hours workaholic Joe would put in, (he ruined his eyes from looking at films), he had to get the approval of not only his staff, and McCoy, but the President of the school and the Board of Trustees.

Penn State's historical roots were Pennsylvania Dutch and Protestant. Byzantine Joe knew what he had to do. Football was easy; he had everyone's respect as a coach. But as an Italian Catholic from Brooklyn, who was a bachelor, and who had early Democratic ties in a Republican state, he would have to be a paragon of a coach.

When McCarthy was on his rampage and was trying to promulgate a public paranoia towards communism, Joe refused to sign a "Loyalty Oath" that McCarthy wanted to have implemented in colleges. At first, he met a little criticism, but when Congress and the public turned on McCarthy, Joe was approved and respected. Joe was and is a conservative liberal, but he leaned toward the Democratic party, probably because of prior association. Joe and his good friend, Bill Hundley, who became Bobby Kennedy's assistant at the Justice Department, and who was a friend of all of the Kennedys, and who eventually became a famous criminal attorney, were the bright young men in the neighborhood. Hundley's father had died when he was young and my Dad recommended him to Fordham Law School. My father really liked Bill Hundley.

As the Democratic party disintegrated from liberalism to permissiveness, Joe switched to the Republican party and later became friends with two presidents, Reagan and Bush. Joe, however, is conservative with liberal feelings for all people. There is a big difference from being a liberal, (most religious leaders over the years could be so classified) than being permissive in the mores and family values, etc. However, one must admit, changing to the Republican party probably helped Joe in gaining his job. Someone once asked me if I thought Joe was a genius. My stock answer is football coaches aren't geniuses, though some are extremely intelligent. To me a genius would be a DaVinci, Michaelangelo, Einstein, Bach, or Beethoven; people who create. If Joe has any genetic trait approaching the genius level, it would be his ability to think out and plan to gain his objectives. Being a member of the Republican party certainly was a big step on a ladder to the top.

During those years, I too was busy. Shortly after Dad died, we moved (again) to 31st Street and Avenue P. Mom refused to continue to live in the house on 29th Street. She was totally unreasonable and she talked of ghosts. When I told her we had a nice house with good neighbors, it had no effect. We bought a house with a Certificate of Occupancy for an upstairs apartment on 31st Street and Avenue P. I used the money from the sale of the 29th Street home as a down payment. It looked like a pretty good deal. I would rent the upstairs to help pay the mortgage, and obviously I also would pay rent. Mom only had her monthly veterans check for income, and I had taken Dad's pension money out as a lump sum option and invested in the market, and we did okay, but I still intended to rent the upstairs.

With Cissy being married, the following November after Dad's death, I was totally alone with Mom. I felt it was ironic that I, the son who had been somewhat of an emotional whipping post, had inherited the responsibility of taking care of a mother I wasn't especially close to when growing up, and Joe, the favorite, was free to pursue his life. I felt that I was honorbound to Dad to properly handle the situation that fate bestowed on me. But it was tough. Mom would not let me rent the upstairs to a stranger at a good rate, so I rented to my Aunt Mary and my Uncle George, her brother and sister. They shared two bedrooms, a kitchen and a bathroom. Aunt Mary, a widow, worked at sewing clothes in New York. My Uncle George was on a veteran's pension, didn't work, and was totally unreliable. He was extremely intelligent, but being the youngest in the family with seven sisters, he was horribly spoiled.

To make everyone comfortable, I put a bed in a semi-finished basement and lived there next to the furnace. I used the bathroom on the main floor. I lived like that for several years. I was still on the police department working in the 77th precinct in the Bedford Stuyvesant area in Brooklyn, New York. The pressure of the job and living with Mother and her siblings was bringing me to a breaking point.

Sometimes on my time off, especially on weekends, I would go to the local hangout, Tina's Italian Restaurant on Avenue U and 18th Street. All of the St. Edmund's crowd went there. It was an Italian restaurant run by three brothers; Larry was the oldest, the bartender and Maitre d' and an overall great guy, Gerry was the fat chef, and Al, the third brother, did both jobs. Joe used to be part of the group. Again, strangely enough, most of our friends and the clientele were Irish.

Time and time again, Mom would call while I was there and ask me to drive her and her sisters or friends to different places. At first I acquiesced, but later I stood my ground and said no. Eventually I would be admonished. I never told Joe, and he seldom called to inquire how things were going. I was all alone. Joe was in Pennsylvania, and Cissy, after her marriage, had moved to a nice apartment in Flushing. She was a newlywed, still young, but she tried to help. She had a right to get her marriage off to a good start, so I tried to keep Mom away from her. Newlyweds and talented children shouldn't bear the responsibility of widowed mothers unless there's no other choice. I was there.

Things at 31st Street had become unbearable. Sometimes Uncle George didn't pay his full share of the rent and Mom and her sisters constantly fought. Aunt Mary was great, she would walk miles to and from the train station to save 50 cents so she could help her only son, Nick. Aunt Mary's husband died when she was young. Often, if I was home around supper, Mom would ask me to go pick up Aunt Mary in my car. I did it willingly, she was outstanding and had the great physical stamina of the Cafiero sisters, and I respected her. When it came to money, Aunt Mary paid every penny. I had loaned her son (my cousin Nick) money. He was married and wanted to buy a house. He, like his mother, paid back every penny. Again, Joe had no knowledge of what was going on. I didn't want to burden Joe with unnecessary problems. He had plans for marriage and his career was picking up speed. Siblings should work together.

Finally, the inevitable happened, and Mom started a fight with Aunt Mary, and also Aunt Loretta, (another widow who I also let move in), and Uncle George. Uncle George stopped paying any rent. Mom then said she wanted to move again, nearer to Cissy. Early on, I alluded to my Mother's generosity being commensurate with her personal affluence. Being a widow, her affluence had diminished and so did her generosity. I contributed as head of the household and I probably lost money, but what else was I to do?

Mother's demand to move once again drove us to Kew Gardens, Queens, where she would be near her daughter. We rented a large two bedroom, two bathroom apartment on 118th Street. The rent was extremely high and was really a waste. By that time Joe was contributing $50.00 a month and we had Mom's veteran check, and I paid the rest. Again, I had great meals and could write Mom off as head of the household.

I was still with the New York City Police Department working in the 77th precinct in the Bedford Stuyvesant area of Brooklyn when I became aware of the severe social problems that affected young people. I guess I realized that education was the proper antidote. Consequently, I left the patrol force and went into the JAB—the Juvenile Aid Bureau and worked with youth gangs. That experience made me appreciate what St. Augustine said: "The difference between a great saint and a sinner is direction." Now I knew that someday I would become an educator.

Mary Ellen was still in the picture. She had a good job with the William Morris agency, (later to become an executive), and so I spent a great deal of time hanging out in New York frequenting the best places. Most important, I began to know who I was, no longer was I afraid of women. When Dad dropped dead in my arms, everything began to get clear. I knew why I had then underlying feelings to be free of society's conventional hypocritical platitudes and morals.

The closest male to me, my Dad, a prince, the quintessential American good guy, the perfect father who worked like a dog his whole life for the family's benefit, dropped dead months before he could retire. There would be no dividends of any kind, no leisure time, no excessive income, no grandchildren. Dad did not see one child married or Joe's future great success.

His death had a devastating impact on me, and I decided I wasn't going to worry about conventions and the system. My genetic instincts were to be free of constraints like some of Dad's family. Society would not dictate to me. I was free, free at last. My hangups and complexes disappeared like dusk fleeing the morning sun. I had only to give Mom the proper and reasonable time to be self-sustaining. My interests expanded to food and wine, and, after Mary Ellen, meeting some of the most interesting people in New York, I wasn't a bon vivant, but I was becoming a pseudo gourmet and oenologist. But I still had Mom to take care of. Then came Joe's call about coming to Belmar to meet Sue.

I got to Belmar a little early. We were to meet Joe and Sue at the place where she worked. They weren't there so I got a table outside on the veranda overlooking the ocean.

Mom and I waited. While waiting, I looked out toward the ocean and saw Sue and Joe swimming. Could this be my intense, serious, undemonstrative brother? He and Sue were cavorting in the surf like two young dolphins. He was really hooked. As I watched them get out of the water, and come toward Mom and me, Joe waved and Mom was inscrutable.

Joe and Sue sat down and Joe made the proper introductions. Sue was natural and quite charming. I am sure she had been pre-warned not to overreact to anything Mom said. A waitress came and we all ordered hamburgers and beer, except Sue. She ordered a burger but with a Coke. After the normal amenities, Joe said he and Sue were getting engaged to be married. Mom was not ecstatic, but not antagonistic either.

Mom asked Sue a few questions about her family and just tried to be friendly. Joe and I kept quiet and occasionally glanced at each other. We enjoyed the lunch, the sun and the ocean. After lunch, we returned to see Joe's place and I started back with Mom to Queens. On the way home, Mom asked me what I thought and I said I was happy for Joe, and Sue seemed like a nice girl. But I could see an ambivalent look on her face. She knew it was time for Joe to get a wife. Cissy had been married at 18, and although she really didn't want to share Joe with another woman, but she accepted Joe's decision.

Before the wedding date was set, it was Sue's turn to inform her mother of her intent to marry. Sue's Mom, Alma, is a tall, regal-looking woman, by far the most aristocratic of her family. Alma is an open-minded individual but also a protective mother of all of her five children. Alma Pohland met Joe and Sue in New York at a bar in the Waldorf-Astoria. Alma didn't drink, but when Sue informed her she wanted to marry this older Italian man from Brooklyn, she ordered a double whiskey sour, a humorous but true story. Alma and her gentleman husband, Augie, gave their consent, and a wedding date was set. My job was to organize our family to attend the wedding in Latrobe, Pennsylvania. My only knowledge of Latrobe was that it was the home of the famous golfer Arnold Palmer and it produced "Rolling Rock" beer. The Pohlands were numerous and popular in that small town.

After Dad's death, I stayed with the New York City Police Department for three more years. I enjoyed working with young gang members. Then one day I met an old high school teammate of Joe's and mine, Dick Reilly. We all played together on those good Brooklyn Prep teams. Dick was teaching and coaching football at our high school alma mater, Brooklyn Prep. He said that he needed an assistant and asked if I could help him out. I had my hours at the Juvenile Aid Bureau scheduled so I could help Dick practice from 3:00 to 5:00 p.m. It was great fun and I loved the kids. One day, the school's Rector, Father Vincent Watson, SJ, offered me a full-time job teaching economics and working as an assistant football coach. I didn't hesitate, I said yes, because it was what I wanted to do; I really felt comfortable.

I tendered my resignation to the police department and prepared to start my new job at the semester change. Much to my surprise, I got a call from one of the best Police Commissioners in the history of New York City, Mr. Steve Kennedy. Technically, I still had a few vacation days that kept me under the aegis of the police department. Kennedy ordered me to his office and requested that I stay on the job and offered me just about any detective job I wanted. He gave me a week to make a decision, but it wasn't hard. I called and thanked him and began my career as a teacher/coach.

Being back with the Jesuits was great. I taught economics, geography and history. My companion lay teachers were absolutely outstanding and the coaching was therapeutic. The confidence Mary Ellen had instilled in me and finding a vocation I liked gave me hope for a happy future. Although I met some great people while on the police department, I also met some bad ones, (just like in other professions). If Joe could coach, why couldn't I?

I stayed with Dick Reilly and we had two fine football teams. In 1961 we were undefeated, and Dick moved to a public high school system for a great deal more money. He went to East Meadow High School on Long Island. A few months later, I was also offered a teaching/coaching job at W. Tresper Clark High School in Westbury, Long Island, where I became a history teacher and an assistant football coach to Jack Boyle. Once again, I was associated with a very successful program. I did miss the Jesuits and my lay teacher friends, and I especially missed the kids. One in particular was a good-looking, steel-eyed Irish lad named John Dockery. From the first time I saw him, I knew he was exceptional. John is still my dear friend. He married a girl from Ireland named Ann Mulligan, and I am not sure which one I love the most. They have two daughters, Erin and Ciara; I am Erin's godfather. Currently John has his own business and is a well-known sports commentator on television. John played in a Super Bowl with the New York Jets and played for several years with the Pittsburgh Steelers.

I was coaching at this lower level when I organized a caravan of relatives to attend Joe's wedding. Dozens of phone calls had to be made. Joe didn't know the addresses of our relatives and who should be invited to attend. It wasn't easy to consolidate the family to go to a wedding in Pennsylvania and meet Joe's future in-laws. As expected, Joe was a very popular cousin and nephew, but none of our family (outside of Mom and me) had met Sue or any of her family. I thought it could be fun. But for some people from Brooklyn, an excursion into Western Pennsylvania is like visiting another country.

Joe had rented rooms in a local motel outside of Latrobe for his guests to stay in. Going to the wedding was a mix of my Mother's family and Dad's. From Dad's side came Aunt Rose and Aunt Frances. On Mom's side was Aunt Josie, Aunt Nan, and Aunt Loretta, many cousins, and of course our immediate family.

The night before the wedding, the Pohlands had a pre-wedding ceremony at their home. The home was beautiful, it was sitting on a bluff, with a big sunporch in the rear overlooking a pastoral view. All of the Pohlands and their relatives were there. As soon as the introductions were over, the families began to mingle and the tension was lifted. Especially popular was my Aunt Nan and her husband Walter Lankinaw, (a pure German), and their two blond daughters, June and Ann. My Aunt Rose, the linguist, and my Aunt Frances dazzled people with their knowledge, but most of all the Pohland clan was relieved that the women did not wear black dresses, had no baskets on their heads, and weren't fat. Most of the men were educated and successful. During the times of mass immigration in the 1800s, all immigrants were erroneously stereotyped, i.e., Irish were drunks, Chinese were launderers, etc. Once the prevailing society allowed assimilation, the stereotyping and prejudging gradually declined. As the years rolled by and Joe's star started to rise, sometimes the Pohlands forget Joe's family's achievements.

The wedding was a great success and everyone was pleased, including Sue's grandparents, who were probably the most concerned. But what I noticed was that Sue's immediate family seemed to carry a bit of a guilt complex about World War II and the Holocaust. Sue's father fought in the war and the family were not at all like Nazis. In fact, they were totally void of racism or any type of ethnic or religious bigotry. They could be called quintessential Christians. But I guess they were a little ashamed, much like the Italian people were shamed when Mussolini sided with Hitler, and are still ashamed of the Mafia. Distinctly competitive by nature, they too, like Joe, tried harder.

Sue, so much like my Mom, seemed to be the strongest. Sue has a sister called Chickie, also married to an ethnic Italian by the name of Dom Fabrio, and has four brothers, Cappie, Dave, Ed and Michael. Her brothers were all fun-loving and involved in sports. My favorite, her brother Cappie, is like his mother. Cappie lives in Alaska, flies his own plane and has raised a family there.

Over all, the Pohlands were not Prussian Aristocrats but close, bucolic farm people; a mix similar to our own family.

And so it was a good marriage. Joe now had a wife of German descent whose father was Protestant and mother Catholic. He already had become a member of the Republican party. He was beginning to fit the image of a Penn State Coach. Be assured he truly loved Sue, but it almost seemed like destiny was giving Joe a helping hand.

# Chapter Seven

# THE BROTHERS AS COACHES

I n 1964, while teaching and coaching in high school at W. Tresper Clark High School in Westbury, New York, I got a phone call from a coach named Chuck Mills. Chuck had been a very successful coach from a small college in Pennsylvania called Indiana University of Pennsylvania. He had accepted a new position as the head coach of the United States Merchant Marine Academy, a Federal Academy also called King's Point, located in King's Point on Long Island. He needed an assistant and I had been recommended. We met for lunch and I accepted a position as a part-time coach, and I continued my teaching job at Clark High School.

After one year and a disappointing season, Coach Mills resigned, stating it was not the situation he thought it would be when he took the job. Due to the recommendations of Coach Mills, and a coach named Clem Stralka, a former All-Pro from the Washington Redskins and a Hall of Famer, (my line coach), Athletic Director Jim Liebertz appointed me as head coach one year before Joe became the head coach at PSU. But some of Liebertz's political enemies, the assistant superintendent, Captain Victor Tyson, and his political friends, were opposed to my appointment. Later on I would have to do battle with their prejudice and their political cabal.

1965 was a happy year for me. My big brother Joe actually came and watched a practice at King's Point. I was terribly flattered. In my first year as the head coach, the team was 4-4-1. But we had upset Temple in our opening game as a big underdog, and then the next week stopped Wagner's (a small college from Staten Island) 11-game winning streak. Wagner was coached by a Penn Stater and former friend and teammate of Steve Suhey, Bob Hicks. In 1965, there were no Divisions 1, 2, or 3, and no NCAA restrictions on the amount of scholarships given. Temple, Post, Hofstra, Gettysburgh, Wagner, and all of the teams we played not only gave scholarships but were producing pro players. Eventually, I had a few also. Presently, King's Point plays the weakest Division 3 teams around, but still has the same scholarship program. Actually, everybody who goes to a federal school is on scholarship, but some exceptions can be made to get athletes in the academies. So I guess I did a pretty good job.

Also in 1965, when Joe and Sue had their first child, Diana (my goddaughter), I had met a new lady friend, Doris Jackson. After Mary Ellen had died at the age of 37, alone in a Sutton Place apartment, I continued to frequent Manhattan. There was a restaurant and bar on First Avenue and 49th Street called "Knob Hill". It was managed by a fellow called George D'Arcy whose brother Richard was a gay ballet dancer and lover of Oliver Smith, one of the foremost set designers in the world. At Knob Hill I met a guy named Bernie Rowan. Bernie was a graduate of Ohio State and an avid fight and football fan. Bernie was the top attorney for a large insurance company in New York City and had an apartment on 51st and First, and he liked to drink. He also did legal work for the famous fighter, Jake Lamotta, "The Raging Bull". Bernie and I became close friends. All kinds of artistic people used to come in and out, including Tennessee Williams, Oliver Smith himself, Richard Boone, mostly known as "Palladin", and it really was a fun place to be.

Bernie's girlfriend Rita was a fairly  good opera singer and eventually she was on the Ed Sullivan show. Rita and Bernie invited me to a party in Peter Cooper Village. The host was the President of United Parcel Service, and his wife was one of Rita's friends. It was a standard New York City cocktail party, a bit like Capote's "Breakfast at Tiffany's". While the party was going on, the doorbell rang, Rita opened the door and a girl appeared who was a friend of the hostess of the party. She was a divorcee; she was absolutely beautiful, and her name was Doris. She also lived in Peter Cooper Village. Before the evening was over, I knew I had to see her again.

Doris had been married to a wealthy man from Princeton, whose family had large real estate investments in Duchess County, New York. They practically owned it. Her sister had married a wealthy Argentinian named Carlito Green, a powerful land owner. Both Doris and her sister had been big-time models. Doris and I went to a Penn State game shortly after Sue had her first child, Diana. Joe and Sue had just purchased their first house and Doris, who had two beautiful little girls of her own, Cynthia and Diana, helped Sue with the baby. I know for sure that Sue really liked her. Doris had a "Lilith" type of personality, a female who was absolutely enchanting, but was used to the sweet life. When I met her, she was also being courted by a rich businessman named Kassover from Sands Point, who had one of the biggest estates. She had also dated several celebrities from movies, Broadway, and many rich industrialists. After her visit she told me she really loved Joe and his family. Being exposed to Mary Ellen and now Doris, it again dawned on me that there was a new breed of woman in society; beautiful, intelligent people who wanted careers and the better things in life. The little house with the kids and the accompanying basics would not suffice.

Instinctively I knew our relationship would be an ephemeral affair. In her world of riches and nabobs, a coach certainly wouldn't do. Her attraction to me, as was Mary Ellen's, was my total indifference to capitulating to the system to make money. A puzzling problem for people who want to be emotionally involved. When Doris considered marriage to me, her sister flew in from Argentina and destroyed any chance of a ceremony.

Money was the key, but this was the time of Kerouac and Salinger and the Beat Generation was on the move. This was the beginning of Women's Liberation. I guess this new breed of women and my getting a late start in the social world put me on a road to bachelorhood. I have been criticized by some for not being married; my sister-in-law, Sue, thought something was wrong. Joe and Sue have three married children; two  girls, Diana and Mary Kay, 31 and 29, and Jay (Joe, Jr.). Both girls put their careers on hold and decided motherhood could be included with their ambitions. Diana has two boys, Brian, 18 months, and Matthew, four months. And little Mary K has a daughter, "Olivia", 13 months old. We are still  waiting for Jay. Diana and Mary K wanted careers, so maybe I was a little ahead of my time, as were the women I dated.

1966 was an eventful year for Joe Paterno; he finally succeeded Rip Engle, after 15 years as a hardworking assistant. He was happily married with two daughters, Diana and Mary Kay. I had moved to Port Washington on Long Island to be closer to the Academy. I lived on the water and it was only 15 minutes from work. Mom was living in Flushing and Cissy, now residing in Forrest Hills, had remarried in November 1996. Two weeks later, her first husband, Warren, whom she married in 1955, died. Her son, Warren Jr., was living with her since the split. Warren Quaid, her first husband, was sickly when she married him, and he eventually died of bleeding ulcers. They never got along after the honeymoon. He was an only son and came from good parents, but the business world became an insurmountable adversary. There were bad feelings between the Quaids and Cissy, but we did the right thing and went to the wake; another event Joe was lucky to miss.

In 1966, everyone at Penn State expected big things from the team and were waiting to see what this hot shot coach would do. Joe got off to a bad start, he had two wins and three losses after five games. It looked like he was in trouble going into the second part of the season, but he managed to win the remaining games and end up with five wins and five losses, but to say that was a disappointing season would be an understatement. Some Penn State fans began to question the administration's decision to appoint Joe.

On the Saturdays when Joe's team and my team played, my mother would get up early on Saturday and say a Novena, praying that we would win. Maybe she did have some supernatural powers. I too was worried about Joe's first year, after all, he worked much harder than I to get the job, so I wanted him to be very successful. I told my Mom to forget about praying for me. I only had a small college job and Joe was in the big time and she should concentrate her prayers on Joe. Well, it has worked. Joe has won 289 games and is still going strong. I won a total of 47 before I gave up coaching.

In the second part of that 1966 season, to get things turned around, Joe started to play some of his younger players and he became the hard-nosed disciplinarian that he is known as today. It saved the '66 season and was the beginning of what would later be called "The Grand Experiment".

In 1967, Joe and Penn State were 8-2-1, and in '68 and '69, won all of their games; that is 11 for each season. The team had really come about and won 31 games without a loss. Joe was the talk of the coaching world. He had made his first great strides toward what he and his old buddy, Ridge Riley, wanted. Riley was the former Executive Director of the Alumni Association, and author of *The Penn State Newsletter.* He later wrote, with Joe's help, a book called *The Road to Number One.* Riley's idealism and love of sports blended with Joe's Ivy League background and  values. Together they believed a team could become the National Champions and be number one made up of student-athletes. There would be no cheating in academics, no abuse of young athletes, no prostitution of educational values and no exploitation of minority groups; truly a Quixotic endeavor.

The more successful Joe became, the more he got a reputation as an eastern idealist whose iconoclastic attitudes were a danger to the old foundation of collegiate football, euphemistically called "The Good Old Boys", with roots deep in the South.

The '68 and '69 teams were two of the best Penn State ever had and really put them on a higher level. They not only dominated the East, but they were perennially in a bowl game, winning most of them. Penn State football became Joe Paterno. Many on his teams became outstanding pro players and that only embellished Joe's and the school's reputations. It was that success that vindicated his and Ridge Riley's philosophy and put Joe into warp speed. The road to number one was now not only open, but Penn State was capable of transporting the team to the desired end. Instead of easing up on work after the 31-game streak, Joe began to work harder and harder. He was an obsessed man. His first son, David, was born, and Sue took care of their home and the kids. Joe, like Odysseus, was allowed to travel and conquer the monsters in his way.

I was doing well at the Academy, but Joe was distancing himself from me as a brother and coach. Soon, I was to be put into the crucible to make some difficult decisions.

One day in 1967, I met my buddy, Bernie Rowan, in The Knob Hill restaurant. He was with Jake Lamotta, the ex-middleweight champ of the world, and a fellow called Peter Savage. Savage was Jake's old buddy and co-author and advisor on the book *The Raging Bull.* Savage was allegedly connected to organized crime, owning clothing factories, and he had the right connections in the movie industry. Surprisingly so, Pete, without the benefit of an education had writing and directing talents. Pete was in several movies himself, including the "Vallachi Papers." He was a big, good-looking man and was instrumental in getting Dino DiLaurentis to produce the Oscar contending film, "The Raging Bull". Jake didn't make a move without Pete.

Being Bernie's friend, I was accepted as an okay guy. Lamotta was an interesting man. His record as a fighter speaks for itself. Much to my surprise, I was bigger than he was. The facial punishment turned what once was probably a handsome youth into a beaten-up warrior, but he had big dimples and a nice smile. Jake's most glaring physical characteristics were his chin and short neck. If ever there was a Neanderthal specimen from the shoulders up, it was Jake Lamotta. Paradoxically, he had tiny hands and I fantasized that I could give him a good fight. What was frightening were his eyes. Jake had narrow, beady eyes that burned you when he was angry. He had killer's eyes and soon I was to be in their focus.

One Sunday afternoon, I was having a drink at PJ Clarks, a popular saloon on Third Avenue. I was with an Asian girl named Katsume, who was half Japanese and half Korean. She was very tall and her hair was black as a raven's wing, with alabaster skin covering her high cheek bones. Her sister Konoko was alleged to be the mistress of Yul Bryner, the famous movie and stage star. Katsume was as delicate and refined as porcelain and was married to a sea captain who was away for long periods of time. While visiting the academy, we were introduced and I asked her for a date, not knowing her marital status. She eventually told me, and we were in the process of terminating the relationship when Jake walked in.

Jake was accompanied by a young girl of about 25. I had seen Elizabeth Taylor close up at the Blue Angel bar and night club just before she took up with Eddie Fisher. The girl with Lamotta surpassed Elizabeth Taylor for pure beauty. It was a full bar at PJ's, but when Jake came in with his escort, everyone put their glasses down and looked at them. The woman Lamotta had with him was a unique beauty. She had gorgeous auburn hair and large violet eyes. Her looks could be described as a mix of Elizabeth Taylor and Jacqueline Bissett. She wore a summer blouse and slacks, and tried to hide what seemed to be the perfect figure. She was Australian and her name was Lynn Tricky.

Jake was in his glory as every eye turned toward him, and he immediately came over to me. He had met and ogled Katsume before, and in his way he was saying, "Top this, Pal". Jake looked like the miner who found an exceptional stone. For the first time, I saw Jake buy a drink. His date had orange juice. The woman demurely and shyly gave all of her admirers the once over. Her looks gave her commanding confidence but she really didn't flaunt her advantage. Jake proudly introduced Lynn to several people and tried to create the illusion that this was his new love. The girl was in total control, explaining to all that she had just met Jake at the Pickwick Arms Hotel and he was nice enough to ask her out for a drink in a strange city. She told us she was from Australia via New Zealand and Canada. Her demeanor was cold but honest. We all understood Jake was nothing but a brief acquaintance. Before an hour had passed, at least seven males came over to say hello. Then within two days, everyone called her for a date, including me. Little did I know what future effect my call would have on my life.

Between 1955 and 1962, when Joe got married, once in a while he would call home, and if he was recruiting near the area, he would come to visit Mom. He knew I was living with Mom and Cis was helping out, he took advantage knowing Mom was being cared for, but Cis and I understood.

After Joe got married and began his journey to fulfill his mission, we seldom heard from him and the only time he saw Mom was when he combined a visit with a recruiting trip. Mom would get excited because Joe was coming. I had to go out and buy all the foods he liked: artichokes, peppers, eggplants and more. Also, I had to pick him up and after his recruiting visit, take him to Mom's and then back to his hotel. It wasn't a big deal and I didn't mind, but you could tell he was growing more and more distanced from our family. In fact, after a couple of Bowl games during the holiday season, I would have to remind him to call Mom and wish her a Merry Christmas or a Happy New Year. He was always happy that I reminded him. The problem was, he would concentrate so much on the game that he would forget everything else. It bothered me a bit but I tried to understand. Was Joe becoming too self-centered? After all, Sue's family was always there, and as the years went on, it got worse.

In 1969, after an undefeated season, Joe took Penn State to the Orange Bowl to play a tough Missouri team that was 10 and 1. Just after Penn State had decided for the Orange Bowl, Michigan upset Ohio State, then ranked number one. It looked like Penn State could and would be voted number one.

But then President Richard Nixon was advised by a former popular coach, Bud Wilkinson, (who had political ambitions), and who was a TV color analyst, to claim the winner of the Texas-Arkansas game as National Champion. Texas was ranked number two. Actually Nixon, a Republican, bought Wilkinson's strategy that he could gain the support of some Southern Democrats. But Penn State had gone 31 games without a defeat, and Arkansas was only ranked number 6. The rest is history. Penn State beat Missouri, Texas beat Arkansas, and Nixon put his foot in his mouth and declared Texas number one.

All hell broke loose in the State of Pennsylvania. Governor Schaeffer, also a Republican from Pennsylvania promulgated a formal protest against Nixon's dumb decision. Nixon countered with offering Penn State a special trophy for having the longest winning streak in the country. Joe told the President of the United States to keep his trophy, he already had the winning streak. Plus, he crowned his kids National Champs and gave them rings, claiming he had a better right than Nixon to do so.

Until a team is beaten on the field they shouldn't be voted to an inferior position. Joe Paterno proved to be a smarter and a better politician then Bud Wilkinson. By making a stand for his team, the rank and file of the State of Pennsylvania closed behind him, now he truly was their champion.

# Chapter Eight

# DON QUIXOTE WITH A MACHINE GUN

After the '68-'69 season, and his moral victory over the President of the United States, Joe Paterno became a symbol to the masses who vicariously identified with teams, coaches, and any hero to their liking. Newspaper writers were calling him the new Don Quixote. I had to chuckle. Cervantes' character was a farcical person who attacked the existing evils in society with a lance, knowing that he couldn't win; valor and beauty were his endeavors, not his conquest. Also, Cervantes really wanted to point out the evils that existed in Spain at that time. If Joe Paterno was Quixotic, he was a Don that carried a machine gun. He wasn't tilting at windmills he couldn't conquer. Indeed, conquering was the main and only objective. Don Quixote couldn't compromise without going beyond his moral parameters. Joe might stretch them, but like his attitude toward football, he would bend but not be broken. The mix of his own brilliance and resolve with the public created a Don Quixote image resulting in a coaching force not seen before at such a young age. The old dinosaurs, Woody Hayes, Bear Bryant, Bud Wilkinson, Duffy Daugherty, Bobby Dodd, General Neyland, and Frank Thomas all took years to become football legends. As his career progressed, Joe would challenge many of the imperfections of the existing hypocritical standards within college athletics.

When he came for battle, he was not only prepared, but he was armed. He was not the idealistic romantic, but the idealistic, practical Byzantine. Byzantine Joe would win many victories but also make many enemies. He became more and more a political animal against the counterattacks that inevitably would come. After all, he took on the "Good Old Boys". Some of those with long memories probably cost Penn State the National Championship in 1994, or at least the Co-Championship. As always happens in historic progression, many people get hurt. As Joe became more famous, his political power grew commensurately. Now he was known as a staunch Republican.

During the years of 1968 and 1969, I had become deeply involved with Lynn, the Australian woman that I met with Jake Lamotta. After turning down opportunities to run with a movie crowd and some rich playboys, I felt she was right for me. She had met Joe and Sue, Cissy and her new husband, Phil, and seemed to prefer our style of life.

After two weeks in New York, Lynn had gotten a job with the Australian Embassy. She stayed there for three months and then was hired by Quantas Airlines. She was not a hostess, but a company representative. She quickly rose to the top in her New York division, her picture was in the paper, and she made a good salary and had all of the perks. I eventually would ask her to give it all up and go to cold Michigan State.

One day, when I was picking her up, Jake Lamotta was waiting outside the hotel for both of us. Even though she had only that first date with him, he kind of considered her his girl. She told him that she considered him a friend but she and I were serious. Jake accepted her decision and did not bother us anymore.

In 1969, when Joe had his great year and his joust with Nixon, I had an 8-1 season at the Merchant Marine Academy. Regardless of my success on the field, there was a cabal of administrators and alumni who had powerful political contacts in Washington. The Academy was a quasi-military institution, part military, part civilian. It was under the Department of Commerce, and then later Transportation. When I was coaching, the United States was the number-one maritime nation in the world.

Some of the early students at the Academy were scions of rich maritime families whose fortunes were tied up in the industry. These people had strong political contacts and were prostituting the school for their own personal aggrandizement. Admission to this quasi-military school was different than other academies, because the United States Merchant Marine Academy was not under the Department of Defense, so it was more like a Bureaucratic arm of the Department of Commerce and was a little enclave known by few people outside the shipping industry. There were backdoor ways of gaining admissions for students unqualified in their state, and the Athletic Department was one of those main doors.

Eventually, I would be forced into open combat and would have to fight these political whores. To say the least, even though I was successful, I was unappreciated and everything was made difficult for me. To sustain the program was getting tougher and tougher. The same people who caused my problems were also bitter enemies of my boss, Captain James Leibertz. If Jim Leibertz didn't have the support of former World Championship Boxer, Gene Tunney, (he served with him in the Navy), who had great political contacts also, he would have been ousted early in his career.

Then came a call that would have a dramatic impact on my life. The call was from Francine Daugherty, Duffy Daugherty's wife. She said Duffy wanted to talk to me but was in California for the East-West postseason game, so would I please give him a call at the number she gave me. I was flattered, but I knew the job would have to be as an assistant. Heck, I was a head coach, and even if all the circumstances weren't perfect, I was still the boss. Plus, I had 22 starters back from an 8-1 season and with another good year would have a good chance to get to a bigger school. I didn't want to lose Lynn, so I decided that I would talk to her about my problem.

We met at our favorite place, the bar at the Hotel Carlyle on the east side, a quiet "in" place. I told her that I had a chance to coach at a higher level but would have to move to East Lansing, Michigan. Her answer would be pivotal on any decision I made. If I stayed, I thought we should get married, and if I left for Michigan, I wanted her to come with me. She didn't hesitate. Her reply was that she wasn't sure marriage and children were what she wanted, and she definitely did not want to go to frozen Michigan.

That was it. My macho idealism surfaced; I thought that love was based on the female going wherever the male wanted her to go. Once again it was not to be. Lynn would have to give up a great deal to come with me, but isn't that what true love was supposed to be about? My disappointment and indignation at her decision made me think about Michigan State seriously.

As fortune would have it, the following day Duffy Daugherty himself called. His charm could be felt over the telephone. He said a friend of his who lived in King's Point went to the Academy's games, and concluded that I was a good coach. Duffy then checked me out with Rip Engle, and of course, Rip endorsed me. Duffy said I should at least come to East Lansing for a visit, and I said I would. I thought I would force the situation. Both Lynn and I were sitting on the fence of a tenuous relationship. Maybe Michigan State was the shot that we needed. I told Duffy that I would come.

Prior to going, I spoke to Dick McPhearson and fellow Long Island coach, Joe Scanella at a football convention. McPhearson had been head coach at the University of Massachusetts and went on to great success at Syracuse. After competing against me at CW Post on Long Island, Scanella spent 20 years as an assistant in the pros, mainly with the Los Angeles (formerly Oakland) Raiders. Both advised me against going. They said Duffy was okay, but the rest of the staff were big trouble. Then I spoke to my brother, who I thought might have a soft spot for Duffy because Duffy didn't run the score up in 1966 when MSU clobbered Penn State when Joe was a rookie coach. He thought it could be a good situation, boy was he wrong.

McPhearson and Scanella appeared to be right. I am sure Joe didn't realize that he was recommending me to a program that was the epitome of everything that he and Penn State were against. But Daugherty called again, and I had consented to that visit. A more charming man would be hard to find, but he was in deep trouble, caught between a burgeoning black movement and a racist staff.

Duffy offered me a good deal, a faculty position, which I didn't have at the Academy. I said I would think about the offer. Really, I liked that man, but I knew I would be getting into a hostile atmosphere. The challenge excited me, but the true reason that I eventually accepted was I thought it was time for me to get married and to raise a family, and Lynn or no Lynn, I had to force the issue. Being impetuous and proud, I didn't give her much time. Either she came with me or it was over. Once again, I was childishly idealistic to ask someone to give up so much for me; it was the same with Mary Ellen and Doris. There was a new breed of woman out there; Lynn didn't come and probably it was my fault. Then I knew, at age 39, I probably would never marry. Could it be I was "Larry" from the *Razor's Edge,* destined to pursue unattainable idealism?

# Chapter Nine

# THE BIG TEN

D ue to political pressures at the Academy and my frustrating relationship with Lynn, I accepted the job at MSU in 1969. Of course, I couldn't know I would precede PSU's entrance into the Big 10 in 1993. Was it destiny that I was unknowingly a point scout for Joe? Byzantine mysticism?

My first day on the job at the athletic office was a nightmare. The African-American football players had helped the militant African-American student body take over the Student Union building. In the football office were the white coaches, all MSU graduates. Duffy was out of town. As a new coach on his first day on the job, I wanted to stay out of the interplay. One coach, Gordie Serr, the offensive line coach, (later to become my only white coaching friend), made a feeble effort to diffuse the situation, but he was outnumbered. Fortunately, the police arrived and a major incident was avoided. I asked myself what the hell I had gotten into. How can you have a team when teammates do personal battle based on racism? Before Duffy returned, Gordie Serr filled me in on what was going on.

In the late '60s, the civil rights movement was underway. Martin Luther King, a superb leader, was doing a great job leading the minority African-Americans using Ghandi's tactics. Schools like MSU, Ohio State, Southern Cal and Nebraska were heavily represented by great African-American athletes in football. But there were few African-Americans working for any school in any manner, and most important, there were no African-American coaches. MSU had won two national championships with players like Bubba Smith, George Webster, Clinton Jones, Jimmy Raye, Sherman Lewis, and many others.

The coaching staff was all white and some were racist. Duffy had been criticized for bringing in African-Americans, not only from Detroit, but from the South. Duffy knew all those great athletes weren't allowed in Southern universities, so he brought them to Michigan State. As much a humanist as Duffy was, he didn't worry about academics, because in those days SAT's and NCAA codes didn't exist as they do today, and if they did, no one tried to enforce them. Consequently, MSU probably was the first big-time football school to showcase African-American athletes in a white world. Other Big Ten schools followed to a lesser degree, and then Duffy's good buddy, John McKay from Southern Cal, followed and then Bob Devaney, from Nebraska, a former MSU assistant coach under Duffy. Later, Bill Yeomans from Houston, another former assistant of Duffy's would do the same.

So it was to be expected that MSU would be the first to be confronted by the backlash of the disgruntled African-American athletic community. In 1968 and 1969, a former great African-American athlete, Lamar Thomas, became a leader of not only the African-American athletes, but the African-American student body at MSU. Because of an injury, Lamar Thomas would never play football again. Thomas was a very intelligent leader. He wanted African-Americans on the coaching staff, in janitorial positions and in administrative positions. The all-white MSU assistant football coaches compounded the problem with their attitude. Boy, did Duffy need help. Now I know what he meant when he said he really did need me.

When Duffy returned, he called me to his office and we discussed how to handle the problem. He said he was going to hire Sherman Lewis, an African-American and former MSU great. Sherman was an assistant high school coach in Kentucky, married and with a young son named Kim. Duffy asked me to help break him in and I agreed. When I met Sherman, we immediately became friends. He was inexperienced but very bright. He also was eager to learn and was extremely sincere and personable. Sherman and I spent a great deal of time together. He was treated like a leper by the rest of the staff, except Gordie Serr. For being Sherman's friend, I too was treated like an outcast. Sherman Lewis is today the offensive coordinator of the Green Bay Packers.

In 1969 and 1970, Michigan State had some great individual players, but we weren't really a team, so the combined record of 8-12 was considered poor and the turmoil continued. In 1969 MSU had won their first three games and lost a close game to a great Notre Dame team in South Bend. The defense had fallen apart. Duffy was handling the offense and it was looking good, but the racial problems again surfaced. We had one more good game vs. our state rival, the University of Michigan, coached by Bo Schembechler. MSU beat Michigan, who later won the Rose Bowl.

The following week MSU lost to a poor Northwestern team. That was the pattern for the whole year and also in 1970. Yet, they had great players, including the Saul brothers from Pennsylvania, both outstanding pros. There was also Billy Joe DuPree, another great pro for the Dallas Cowboys, Brad Van Pelt, all pro linebacker with the Giants, Eric Allen, who became one of the top running backs in Canada, and others.

MSU should have had another great squad but the racial division of the team and the arrogance and racism of the staff culminated in mediocrity for Duffy, the team and the program. Duffy would eventually pay for a situation out of control. A few years later he was dismissed.

After the two National Championships at Michigan State, not only had the entire administration and staff become complacent, they had become arrogant. The same thing almost happened to Penn State, but Joe nipped the problem at the bud.

As a bachelor, coaching in a hostile situation in a small town like East Lansing was tough. I really missed Lynn, but that was over. As a guy on the faculty, approaching the coeds, who were not interesting, was also taboo. All the other coaches were married so I was on my own. I always seemed to meet somebody who could make things better. I wasn't the type to frivolously seek female company, and then I met Tove. Tove was a waitress in one of the better restaurants in East Lansing. She was a very natural person. Not beautiful in a classical manner, but with her naturalness and her beautiful hair, she was very striking looking. Tove never wore any makeup, and she could do anything, including extracting syrup from trees. She was a true outdoor person, and I'm sure her Norwegian and Danish ancestors helped settle the Midwest.

But as usual there was a problem. She had three children and was separated from her husband. I finally met a woman who wasn't interested in a career and didn't want to be liberated, who just wanted to raise her family. Once again, I had to make a decision. At age 40, I really didn't want to be the father of someone else's kids; I wanted my own. But fate intervened again.

We had just completed the 1970 season and I was frustrated. One of the alumni from the Merchant Marine Academy, a Mr. Harry Keefe called. He heard I wasn't too happy and he and his friends wanted me to return. The coach, Drew Tallman, the man that I recommended to take my place had resigned. They were prepared to make me an associate professor, the head football coach and the assistant athletic director. It sounded pretty good.

Harry also said that the maritime administrator (the top man) wanted me back and that all my former enemies were under his authority and naturally as politicians they wouldn't dare go against him. His name was Andrew Gibson and he went to Brown when Joe and I played. And Gibson was part of the inner circle of the Republican party.

Tove was another wonderful person whom I had met. The world is full of great people who may never get into the limelight and who sometimes must accept fate's capricious whims. Once again it was time to move on.

# Chapter Ten

# ARE YOU
# JOE PATERNO?

I n 1971, the year of my return to King's Point, Joe and Penn State had rebounded from a 7-3 record in 1970 to 11-1 and a number-five ranking in 1971. More and more he was beginning to be accepted as one of the top coaches in the country. And the Penn State program slowly but surely was improving its reputation and stature. The Grand Experiment was being calibrated to a faster speed. Joe always received good ink, but now his picture was continuously seen in magazines, newspapers and on TV. His eloquence in challenging the ills of major college football found open and willing ears with the more idealistic press. Joe had conquered his first windmill. Over the years, if I recorded how many times I've been asked, "Are you Joe Paterno?" a round figure would be 10,000.

My proud reply was always, "No, I'm his brother, George". Some people didn't believe me but I couldn't control their opinions. Joe and I do resemble each other, but side by side there is a noticeable difference. He always wears thick glasses and is about two inches taller and twenty pounds lighter than I am. But I guess the mind paints itself images of people frequently seen on TV and/or in the press. To tell the truth, after a while it vexes me, especially at Bowl games, where it would happen five to ten times a day, mostly from Penn State fans.

Only once did I ever say I was Joe. Before reporting back East to again coach the United States Merchant Marine Academy, I decided to vacation in Acapulco. Duffy gave me a generous bonus and through a man who graduated from Michigan State's Hotel and Management School, I got a beautiful room in a Holiday Inn.

Subconsciously, I hoped I would bump into Lynn. She had told me about a small hotel frequented by wealthy Australians, British, and some Americans. It was in walking distance, so every day around 4:00 p.m. I took a stroll and went to a little circular bar down by the water. In those days, I was drinking Martinis with a lemon twist, straight up. Between the Beefeater gin and the breeze that came off of Acapulco Bay, it was idyllic. I was so relaxed, devouring the ambiance, that I didn't notice the two couples across the way. While I was looking at the beautiful sunset, a hand touched my shoulder. I looked into the face of a distinguished tall, slim, gray-haired man, and he said "Hi, Joe".

I was so relaxed I didn't feel like going into the old spiel, "Sorry, I'm not Joe, I'm his brother", so I just said "Hi." The stranger said, "Don't you remember me?" I said sure, I can place your face but don't remember your name. Even with my sunglasses on, I could see the man was perplexed. But he continued to be gracious and asked if I would join him and his wife and their friends for a drink. I looked across the bar and there was the stranger's wife and another distinguished-looking couple, also gray haired. It was too late; so I said okay to a drink.

I went with my new friend who had given me a name I certainly didn't recognize. He then proceeded to introduce me to his friends as Joe Paterno, the coach at Penn State. But he still looked confused. I accepted his drink and then he asked me a question that led me further into the web. What was I doing in Acapulco?

Understand now, Joe had four children and I was a bachelor. So instinctively I said Penn State was interested in recruiting a boy from Texas and being out west I thought I would take a peak at Acapulco to see what it was like. In the '70s Acapulco was one of the places for the "Jet Set." What the hell was Joe Paterno doing there alone?

The man's perplexed look became one of consternation. Actually he and his wife and friends were so nice, and I was having a good time, so I bought them a drink. As I was drinking my fourth martini, he said, "Joe, are you sure you don't remember me? I saw you two weeks ago." Again I said he looked very familiar. Then I knew I was in deep trouble. I bid my adieu and went to my hotel in a quandary. Finally I got Joe on the phone the next day. My newfound friend was no other than the President of U.S. Steel and Joe had two weeks prior spoken at an annual dinner for executives for a stipend of $5,000 and I said he only looked familiar. Usually, Joe doesn't swear, but he did call me a stupid S.O.B.

That was the first and only time that I said I was Joe Paterno. Naturally, Joe immediately called and when he made contact, he explained my peccadillo and the man laughed and said he knew it all the time. So no one was offended. But this is a problem I still have to live with. People want to meet famous personalities and some refuse to take no for an answer; another consequence of society's overemphasis on fame marketed by the media.

It's tough enough to live in the shadow of a famous sibling and even tougher when you look like him. On a few occasions, fans from competitive schools tried to pick fights with me. I learned discretion is the better part of valor and would make hasty retreats. Sometimes it's a bit like having a brother who is a famous and feared gunfighter. When you come to town, half the people are afraid of you and the other half want to kill you. But I've survived.

# Chapter Eleven

# TO BE OR NOT TO BE?

A t the end of the 1972 season, 10-2 with a loss to Oklahoma in the Sugar Bowl, Joe had to make a Shakespearean decision. It was the day after Penn State lost to Oklahoma minus their star back, John Cappelletti (out with the flu) that Joe called me in my room. Joe, always going first class, stayed with the team two extra days in New Orleans. He said to meet him in the lobby.

When he came off the elevator he said, "Let's take a walk to the French Quarter." I thought we were headed to the Royal Sonesta Hotel for some clams or oysters and beer. But he told me he was going to meet with Billy Sullivan, the roguish Irishman who owned the New England Patriots. It was then I learned Joe had been in contact with Sullivan before the bowl game. Sullivan had offered Joe the head coaching job with a long-term contract and megabucks.

Sullivan had done his homework. Joe liked the New England area, especially Boston with its intellectual cosmopolitan environment. After all, he went to Brown, and Providence and New York City were so close.

Shrewd Sullivan was planning the Foxboro Stadium straddling Rhode Island and Massachusetts, and both states' populations were loaded with Italian people. Hiring the hottest college coach around in the East who was being compared to Lombardi would be a coup and a wise business decision.

Before reaching the hotel, Joe asked me if I would come with him as an assistant. I said yes. I didn't want to be on his college staff for many reasons, mostly because it may have put added pressure on him, but pro ball was a dog-eat-dog business for money and you needed extremely loyal assistants, people who could protect your backside. Joe told me he had talked to his buddy Jim Tarman, who was then sports information director, about being general manager, so it looked as if he was seriously considering Sullivan's offer.

We arrived at the hotel and he went up to Mr. Sullivan's room. I waited at the bar and had some clams and beer. About an hour and a half passed before Joe came down alone. I asked if he wanted some clams or oysters and he said, "No". We started back to our hotel and that frown I've seen so often appeared. You could practically hear that computer mind evaluating all the data, trying to come to a decision. My curiosity got the best of me and I asked, "Well, what are you going to do?"

He told me that the offer was well over a million dollars guaranteed, plus perks. I thought to myself, if Joe accepts, he would be financially set for life. Joe said he wasn't sure what to do; he would talk it over with Sue (as he does all family matters). He truly had ambivalent feelings, so I dropped the subject. The next day I went to the Academy and Joe and Sue went home to Happy Valley.

Billy Sullivan, a heck of a nice man, had a penchant for publicity; after all, he was a former PR man; he had extrapolated from his meeting with Joe. He thought he had pulled off a great coup and no one could turn down that kind of money. Joe talked to Sue, and they decided the children were young, Sue had roots in the area and financially they were doing okay.

Sullivan was shocked when he received Joe's polite call turning down a million bucks. Sullivan had prematurely released to the papers that Joe had signed the most lucrative contract in the history of the NFL. Dick Young from the *New York Daily News* had a big blurb in his paper.

It was Sunday, and I was having a staff recruiting meeting at the academy. Working for me at that time was a small, brash redheaded Irish kid with freckles. He wasn't the greatest coach, but he was very intelligent and was an outstanding scout. His name was Bill Polian and after working for me for five years, by his own initiative and ability he rose to be general manager of the Buffalo Bills. Polian hired Marv Levy and built the team that went to four superbowls. Currently, Bill is general manager of the Carolina Panthers.

Coming all the way from the Bronx where he lived, to Long Island, often caused Bill to be late. So I started the meeting without him, and the whole staff kidded him about his tardiness. About ten minutes later, Bill came sprinting down the corridor calling my name. When he came into the room, I saw he had a paper with him. Polian said, "You won't believe what I am going to tell you!!" and I replied, "I guess Joe turned the Patriots down". Polian said, "How did you know?" I said, "Joe hasn't finished what he set out to do, and turning down the Patriots would give Don Quixote heavy artillery and a million Sanchos". I was disappointed, but I had come not to expect serendipitous fortune.

During Joe's career he has been approached by not only the New England Patriots but also the Pittsburgh Steelers, the Cleveland Browns and the NY Giants. The owners finally realize that he loves Penn State and Happy Valley, so they don't bother him anymore. Joe didn't become a coach to make money, he became a coach to educate young men.

# Chapter Twelve

# FOOTBALL
# AND POLITICS

I n 1973, there was a staff change in assistant coaches. The backfield coach, George Welsh, a former great quarterback at the Naval Academy, left to lead his alma mater back to prominence. Welsh, one of the top coaches in the country, is still active at the University of Virginia. Joe and Sue and George and his wife Sandra became and still are close friends. But as always, fate came to Joe's assistance and he hired Dick Anderson from the Lafayette team that was one of my opponents. Joe replaced quality with quality and maybe Dick was a better recruiter than the phlegmatic Welsh. Bob Phillips, one of the first coaches Joe hired in '66 moved up to backfield and quarterback coach, so Joe's staff remained talented and solid.

In 1969, the professional Pittsburgh Steelers, owned by the venerable Art Rooney, had fallen on bad times, and he had preliminary negotiations with Joe Paterno. He had offered Joe the job, but Joe never seriously considered taking it. He spoke to Mr. Rooney out of respect, but considering the Steelers' situation and his own, he had no problem saying no. 1969 was the same year Joe decided to stand up to President Nixon and turn down the Steelers job. Those decisions added to the

1972 decision to turn down a million-dollar pro contract with the Patriots, solidified his reputation to such a degree that he began to attract fans nationwide. Joe had become a favorite of writers and fans after the '67 season, but now with the newly added luster, politicians started to woo him, wanting his support.

Governor Raymond Schafer, who had preceded Governor Milton Schapp, had always been an active supporter, but now Congressmen and Senators wanted pictures with Joe: moreover, the local politicians acted like vassals. Byzantine Joe played the situation perfectly; the swarthy young "dago" from Brooklyn was becoming a political force in the state of Pennsylvania. Amazing!!

After turning the pro jobs down in '69 and '72, Joe received a substantial raise with perks and great leverage against a few Penn State administrators who thought he was moving too fast. Dr. John Oswald had replaced Dr. Eric Walker in 1970 as the president of the school. Ed Czekaj had replaced Ernie McCoy as the athletic director. Czekaj was a former Penn State player who participated with Steve Suhey in the 1947 Cotton Bowl tie vs. Southern Methodist (SMU). Czekaj's signature was his great golf game and his outrageous paisley jackets. Joe could see the light at the end of the tunnel. There would be no stopping him. He was approaching Bear Bryant and Bud Wilkinson as football coaches with political clout.

The '73 team was a veteran group led by a great tailback, John Cappelletti; a super defensive tackle, Randy Crowder; and an offensive guard, Mark Markovich. The team won 12 games and lost none, ending with a victory over LSU in the Orange Bowl game. Once again, Penn State didn't get its just due; PSU was voted fifth in the national polls with no National Championship, just like the '68 and '69 teams which went 22-0 and yet did not win the National Championship.

Was it anti-Joe Paterno or anti-Eastern football? How could Penn State's allegedly weak schedule be so weak, if they could beat the best teams in the country in Bowl games? Another slap in the face for Penn State University and the state of Pennsylvania. The Midwestern and the Southern teams with

Notre Dame had always been in contention for the national title. Many people said "the good old boys" didn't want this "wop" to prove you could be a National Champion with his rebellious attitudes toward the existing NCAA structure. After all, in the South they were beginning to use African-Americans.

The polls didn't respect Penn State, but other, more open-minded experts did. John Cappelletti, the great tailback whose accomplishments caught the country's imagination won the coveted Heisman Trophy in 1973. It was an event in Heisman history that soon would be recorded for posterity.

An organization called the Downtown Athletic Club, "DAC" was and still is the sponsor of the Heisman Trophy. The president was Mr. Neil McAllister, scion of the McAllister tugboat clan; a fellow student at Brooklyn Prep and a friend of Joe's. The voting for the Heisman Trophy is nationwide, so Neil might have been a Penn State rooter, but not a factor. But he did set a stage for one of the most memorable evenings in the illustrious history of the Heisman Dinner.

John Cappelletti could have modeled for a statue of Adonis. He was a big, powerful athlete, gifted with swiftness and stamina. But this sensitive noble warrior carried a heavy heart on the night he was to receive college football's most prestigious award. His younger 13-year-old brother Joseph was suffering from incurable Leukemia. The night of the dinner, Joe and the Penn State administration had a pre-dinner cocktail party for the Cappelletti family and all their friends and Penn State friends. Little Joey was there, and I am sure he didn't know how ill he was, but the pride and love for his big brother John glowed in his eyes. The spiritual bond between little Joey and his big brother John was so palpable that it gave everyone present a warm feeling. Mr. and Mrs. Cappelletti, bursting with pride for John could not fully rejoice, knowing Joey's situation. What beautiful people. They masked their intense sorrow with happy smiles in honor of John.

Award dinners, including the Heisman's, are usually boring. You have generic guest types who make redundant remarks and the accolades are the same ones used every year.

But not this night. John Cappelletti's acceptance speech was a classic, never to be forgotten. It reminded all who attended what sports, football and the Heisman dinner were all about.

The dais was a mix of distinguished politicians, athletes and media moguls. Because of my Brooklyn Prep relationship with McAllister and the fact that the DAC was a watering hole for the maritime industries, as the head coach of the USMMA, I was seated on the dais. Next to me and my companion for the evening was the famous Bishop Fulton Sheen. When Milton Berle was dominating TV, his biggest competitor was Bishop Sheen. He was a worthy opponent for Uncle Milty.

For the first time, the dinner was taken out of the Downtown Athletic Club facilities because a larger dining hall was needed. It was a typical major sports dinner. The emcee was humorous, and there were brief talks by many former famous players effusive in praise for what football did for them and their congratulations for Cappelletti. Homage was also given to all the former Heisman award winners. As we progressed through the courses served, Bishop Sheen and I were getting friendly. Only twice before had I looked into such penetrating eyes, Father Thomas Birmingham, S.J., and Lynn's, and at the risk of sounding trite, I would have to say Sheen's eyes were dazzlingly hypnotic. No wonder Uncle Milty had to check his TV ratings.

Finally the time came for the presentation of the award. A trio of people spent several minutes praising John Cappelletti and why he was a worthy recipient. John came up to make his acceptance speech. Sitting directly in front of the podium was the entire Cappelletti family with Little Joe directly in front. The boy's eyes were fixed on his big brother, his neck was craned back to see up, and his smile went from ear to ear. If ever a brother loved a big brother, this was the quintessential manifestation. John Cappelletti began his talk. He thanked everyone responsible for the award and the wonderful evening. He spoke of the camaraderie with his teammates and thanked Joe Paterno for his coaching and guidance. Then this big, extraordinary athlete broke down; he had to look directly into the eyes of his dying brother who had little time left. And then he proceeded to bring the entire audience to tears as he sobbingly dedicated the trophy to his little brother. Between sobs he told the audience how his dying brother had shown more courage living day to day in his terminal condition than he had ever shown playing college football. Believe me, there was not a dry eye in the room, including the distinguished sophisticated dais. Even Bishop Sheen's angelic blue eyes were coated with tears. When Cappelletti finished, not a sound could be heard for about a minute; then there was a standing ovation. Bishop Sheen stepped up to the podium to close the dinner with a prayer. He said there would be no need for his prayer, that John Cappelletti's speech was not only a prayer, but a blessing.

After the event, we went to a post dinner party sponsored by the Downtown Athletic Club. The president of the Downtown Athletic Club, Neil McAllister, joined Joe and me and several other people. I said the evening had to be one of the best Heisman dinners ever. Neil said it was, but it was to expected. After all, you had an Irish producer (McAllister) and an Italian cast (Paterno and Cappelletti); humorous but poignant. Joey Cappelletti died six weeks after the dinner, and subsequently Mary Tyler Moore Productions made a well-received movie called "Something for Joey".

Things were going well for me and the team at the academy. The new superintendent, Admiral Arthur Engel (retired from the Coast Guard and former superintendent of the Coast Guard) who grew up in Grand Rapids, Michigan with Vice President Gerry Ford was a staunch Republican. And his boss was our friend Andrew Gibson, the head honcho of the Maritime Administration. I was treated with kid gloves. But I bemused to myself what would happen if the political balance of power abruptly changed. When Joe began to endorse Pennsylvania Republicans and socialize with them, I said, "Hey, Joe, if something goes wrong in Washington, you're an untouchable, but I'm a federal employee". Sometimes Joe doesn't understand how petty and vindictive the lower echelon of bureaucrats can be if they gain a position of power. P.J. O'Rourke wrote a book called *Parliament of Whores,* which if true, then the infrastructures of many of our bureaucracies, especially the Maritime Industries, are rife with obsequious, fawning pimps. Joe's reply to my question was "not to worry". It was at that time when his excursions into the political arena planted a seed that later blossomed to make him consider running for governor of Pennsylvania. It would be a natural lateral move; he would still have notoriety and power and when he achieved his "Grand Experiment", he could take his mission to a higher level. Without a doubt, he thought he could succeed.

Just before Watergate broke, my protector, Andrew Gibson, moved to another government job. His replacement was a man named Robert Blackwell. Although a Democrat, he had become a friend of King's Point's strongest political ally. The man was Milt Nottingham, a rich powerful shipping broker who had no use for football and especially no use for me. War clouds were gathering. Nottingham had contacts with powerful politicians from both parties and was able to help Blackwell to obtain the Maritime's Administrator position.

My supervisor and friend, Captain James Leibertz, Athletic Director, retired (maybe he foresaw what was coming). A man named Dr. Al Negratti, a former pro basketball player, got the job. He was absolutely a great person—a true professional loaded with ability and integrity. Negratti quit within six months after a clash with the acting dean, Paul Krinsky. Krinsky was an alumnus like assistant superintendent Victor Tyson. Nottingham attended the academy on two different occasions, never graduating but was given the title "honorary alumnus". In some ways, he ran the academy because of his Washington contact, and being a superb politician he wanted his own men on the inside. Within a week after Negratti left, a man called Buck Lai, who left a neighboring college, C.W. Post, under bizarre conditions was hired. Lai had a reputation from Long Island University as a baseball and basketball man. He was also known for not wanting coaches to get faculty tenure. While at C.W. Post, he was involved in a tenure dispute with their football coach, Dom Anile, currently director of personnel for the Carolina Panthers.

Before leaving, Negratti (who liked me and thought I deserved tenure) warned me that Tyson and Krinsky were going to surreptitiously try to block my application for tenure. With Nottingham and Blackwell backing them and with a new athletic director whose past record spoke for itself, it didn't look good for George Paterno.

Admiral Engel was still on my side, but his Republican backing was crumbling. He knew the alumni and Nottingham wanted him out and an alumnus in as a superintendent. But Engel had character and was a man of his word. He appreciated a good coach, and he ordered the acting Dean Krinsky to approve my request for tenure and then he signed his approval. The only person who could overrule him was the Assistant Secretary of Commerce, the Maritime Administrator Robert Blackwell. And unfortunately for me, the Watergate scandal broke.

When Watergate broke in 1974, the foundation of the Nixon administration began to shake. Most Republicans in Washington began looking over their shoulders. Probably without Watergate, my tenure process would have been summarily approved, which at that time was the norm. But suddenly there was a mystifying delay. According to the academy's faculty union and civil service regulations, if you served five years, you automatically would get tenure. Not only was I approaching my fifth year, but had been enthusiastically recommended by the superintendent (equivalent to the school's president).

After going through the entire tenure process, no approval was forthcoming from Washington and the Civil Service Commission. Naturally I knew what the delay was. Blackwell had to perfunctorily approve or say no; he was watching the Watergate fiasco. He allegedly said, "Let him hang and twist in the wind." By then I knew all the shallow mundane political idioms. They also used the word "Stonewall" if they were requested to give a truthful response. Bureaucrats always look for procedural loopholes, so technically they could make me wait till the last day of the fifth year. The battle was on!!!

I decided to force the issue and make Nottingham and Blackwell show their hand. Joe called Senator Hugh Scott from Pennsylvania, one of the senior and most powerful Republicans, to intervene. Information was delivered to Scott, it showed I had been approved by the school's tenure committee (made up of peers) the dean and the superintendent (president of the school), normally a de facto approval. Why was my approval being held up by the Maritime Administrator, Robert Blackwell? When Senator Scott put some pressure on Blackwell for the truth, all hell broke loose. Blackwell, taking advantage of the pending Watergate investigation and with great indignation, began to accuse Senator Scott of gratuitous political pressure.

Joe was shocked when told Scott could do nothing. The next step was a request by the Assistant Secretary of Commerce of Pennsylvania, a Mr. James Tabor, to seek justice on my behalf. But as the Watergate scandal worsened, the Democrats in Washington developed a cavalier attitude toward any pressure from the Nixon administration. Blackwell refused to make a decision, and then the Republican house of cards fell in on Richard Nixon, something I honestly felt he deserved.

The alumni at the academy became polarized; sides for Blackwell and Nottingham were getting a lot of heat from the rank and file who wanted a good football program. A counter offer came from Blackwell; he would give me a contract for five years at the same salary I would have received as a faculty member, but with no fringes and no tenure. The atmosphere was overwhelming and was easily traced to the acting Dean Krinsky and the athletic director Buck Lai who were suborned by Blackwell to make this decision.

It was then I thought about my father. A year before he died he was a candidate for a magistrate judgeship. He had 30 years in the courts and all the existing judges not only liked him but depended upon his expertise. Court clerks have vast knowledge of the legal intricacies and most would have backed him. Dad was an active Democrat, and it looked like he had a good shot at his dream. Oh how this man, who thrived on the law and the law books wanted the job. But then the call came. If he wanted to be a viable candidate, $10,000 would be needed up front. There were enough people with money who backed Dad, but Pat Paterno, the idealist, didn't feel a man should have to buy a job, especially a judgeship. While he fought a conflict between ambition and compromise, he received another call. He surreptitiously was told the judgeship was his if he allowed himself to be sponsored by a certain Italian organization. The organization had underworld contacts who wanted an Italian to get the judgeship (not an uncommon occurrence in American politics). Of course Dad said no. No to compromise. No to his lifelong goal. After he died, I wondered how much the disillusionment and despair he suffered had an effect on his death. So I told Blackwell no. Andrew Gibson appointed me, not him, and I was approved for tenure on merit. That's when Joe, after all his earnest endeavor on my part, realized powerful political friends would extend themselves only commensurately to the political climate.

As impeachment talk began concerning Nixon, his Republican friends were looking for a cop-out for themselves. I was expendable. Joe was a big shot who couldn't help, but he also didn't want to jeopardize the excellent contacts he had made; he knew things would change. Nixon resigned. Ford took over. Democrats were having a heyday.

Admiral Engle, the superintendent of the school, was temporarily transferred to Washington and my tenure was overruled by Robert Blackwell and I was out of a job. But Dad would have been proud of me. The fun was just about to begin. For the second time in my life, Joe had implied I was a good guy but would have to learn to bend. I didn't bend, like millions of other people in the world don't bend. Eventually I would be rewarded with a major victory.

Nineteen seventy-four was another good year for Joe Paterno and Penn State, a 10-2 season with a win over a southern team, Baylor in the Cotton Bowl. But once again, only a number-seven national ranking. Don Quixote was treading water, his opponents were filling the moat with crocodiles, and he had to regroup and find ways to advance. But at least he was working. Ford would be out and Carter was the new president.

Joe and all his political Republican friends couldn't help me now. It looked like a dead issue. In 1975, I had won seven games and lost two, was voted coach of the year by our conference and still was terminated. All kinds of excuses were given to the press. I was not academically qualified to be associate professor (I had a written waiver from Mr. Andrew Gibson) or coaches weren't teachers and therefore couldn't be given tenure. The coaches not being teachers quote really shook up the coaching community. They did leave me hanging in the wind, but I didn't die, and once again Joe must have felt the ghost of my mother (he didn't realize I no longer needed him). Joe offered me a job on his staff, and according to Joe, all his assistant coaches came to him and said they wanted me. I doubt if that's true. I turned him down for two major reasons: It wouldn't be a healthy situation for him, and I was determined to fight back. I had filed an appeal to the Civil Service Commission. Carter or no Carter, I wanted justice and damn the torpedoes.

Nineteen seventy-six would be a strange but rewarding year for the brothers Paterno. As I stated, after my 1975 season at the academy, I was terminated for political reasons. Even though my teams had accumulated the most victories in the school's history against the toughest competition with the best percentage of wins per year, I had to apply for unemployment. Probably I was the first Paterno to stand in the unemployment line. Dad must have turned over in his grave. Because of my financial situation and an unknown future, I had to give up my nice apartment and move to a lesser area where I paid a lower rent. The existing pressures led me to once again read *The Razor's Edge*. When depressed in his search for the truth, the main character, "Larry" turned to meditation. So I purchased several books on Yoga, Buddhism, Hinduism, and dove into a sea of transcendental meditation. Between meditation and reading, I became quite sure I did the right thing.

In 1975, Penn State had upgraded its schedule, adding Stanford, which had a great team. Stanford's two great wide receivers were Tony Hill and James Lofton who became All-Pros. Their quarterbacks, Benjamin and Cordova, also became pros. Ohio State was also added with its great fullback, Pete Johnson. Kentucky and a powerful North Carolina State team coached by Lou Holtz and also a strong rejuvenated Pitt team were added. The team played great football and went 9-3, losing a close game to top-ranked Alabama in the Sugar Bowl. But again, Penn State was only ranked tenth in national polls. But Joe had made his point. Penn State was playing one of the top schedules in the country and more than held their own. People were beginning to take serious notice. Playing tough teams like Stanford, Ohio State, Iowa, Kentucky, North Carolina State and Alabama could not be called a weak Eastern schedule. Byzantine Joe was setting a trap for the future.

My official termination came in 1976, and I immediately filed an appeal. Most of the correspondence had to go to Washington so I decided to contact our old family friend Bill Hundly. Bill Hundly became a famous and highly regarded lawyer in D.C. After rising to the position of Robert Kennedy's right hand man in the Justice Department, Bill decided to go to the other side after the Kennedys were assassinated and Nixon was elected. Bill became one of the top defense lawyers in Washington, and although a Democrat, John Mitchell, the Attorney General, and the Secretary of Commerce Stans asked Bill to defend them concerning the Watergate scandal. He did so admirably. Later, Nixon himself requested Hundly's aid concerning the demand for his private tapes. Bill turned the president down. He told me his two liberal daughters threatened not to talk to him if he took the case.

Bill Hundly was a six-figure lawyer, and he knew I couldn't afford him, but he told me to come to Washington. When I explained my predicament he chuckled, saying I hadn't changed. And Bill felt he could help me with a few phone calls. After all, he was famous and a powerful Washington lawyer with many political contacts. But then he added he would take the case on one condition, which was he didn't want to be paid. When I objected, Bill replied he was "paying Dad back". If I wanted to give his young assistant Corey Middleman, a small stipend, that would be okay. Middleman was to do the necessary paperwork in my appeal. That's the kind of man Bill Hundly is. After a nice lunch he sent me back to Long Island with a warm feeling. He would be in touch in a few days.

About three days went by and I got my call. "George," Bill said, "This is going to be tougher than I thought. They really want your ass. But let's proceed, it should be fun." Bill hated the ruthless, arrogant power-mad bureaucrats. He also said I had a great case and that my due process was egregiously violated. Then he gave me the old Hundly chuckle and said, "They shouldn't pick on guys from Brooklyn".

Under the best conditions, government legal matters in Washington move slowly, but when a bureaucracy stonewalls proceedings (knowing they are wrong) movement practically comes to a halt. We understood and we refused to be discouraged.

My appeal was filed and a few months went by with me collecting unemployment insurance, reading and meditating. I thought of the '76 football season that was coming up. Suddenly a few things happened in a space of a few weeks.

A month prior to the football season, I received a call from a Mr. Nelson Goldberg, a resident of Fox Hills, Pittsburgh and an owner of a company called TCS. Mr. Goldberg was a graduate of Penn State and as a student, a friend of young assistant coach Joe Paterno. Joe really liked Nelson, he reminded him of a former neighbor and still a friend, Frank Mastiloni. Goldberg was a charming huckster like Mastiloni, extremely smart and skilled in his profession, which was radio and TV.

In 1975, Joe had intensified the severity of the football schedule so he knew he had to broaden his recruiting base to reach more kids. Nelson saw the opportunities for the future, he believed in Joe, and they had a great rapport. So in 1975, TCS had a cable TV show of Penn State's games with hopes of selling them locally and in other parts of the country where viewers didn't know who and what Penn State was about. Nelson hired the venerable Ray Scott to do the announcing. Scott was a major talent with a big time name. Scott's assistant was the colorful Max McGee from the great Green Bay teams coached by Vince Lombardi. Scott was the voice of Green Bay in their glory days and one of the top announcers in the business.

Hiring Nelson was part of Joe's plan to complete the "Grand Experiment". Nelson was a willing volunteer, he loved Penn State and Joe and knew he could possibly make big bucks. In '75 the TV show was seminal, not totally received by the audience. In Pennsylvania, people are not easily impressed and are very slow to commit themselves to anything. Just as early on they were slow to approve of Joe as their coach.

When I received Nelson Goldberg's call, he said Max McGee would not be available to do the color for the '76 games and would I be interested in taking his place? I was caught totally by surprise. When coaching my teams, I couldn't go to Bowl games or playoff games, so I went to Penn State's. On many occasions, I spent social times with Mr. Goldberg and his beautiful and charming wife Marcia. He was a fun guy. Although I knew Nelson and had talked football with him, I couldn't see myself replacing Max McGee, and the idea of working with Ray Scott frightened me. Also I smelled Joe's influence in the background. So in response to Nelson's offer I said I would come to Pittsburgh and talk, but if I accepted his proposition, I would have to be my own man and say what I thought was objectively correct. Upon my return from the interview in Pittsburgh, I signed a contract with TCS. The money was meager, but I was promised my individuality. Most important, I felt good about being involved with Penn State football. I could see the games and maybe make a small contribution. After all, I was out of work, waiting for a decision on my appeal. Joe and I would be together again. The Corsican Brothers would be tough to beat.

Nelson Goldberg probably was apprehensive about a neophyte in the TV business. I'm sure he wanted to placate Joe and was dreaming of future endeavors. He didn't know at that time that he launched me into a media career that has lasted over 20 years. Maybe we all thought that it would be for one year, and he unknowingly created a "Frankenstein". I don't know. But I couldn't have hurt them too much, because Penn State has won two National Championships and should have won a third in my tenure. Nelson's not around anymore and I probably won't be in the near future.

The second call I received was from my lawyer, Bill Hundly. I had started my new job as color analyst for Penn State. Bill had good news. He said he had been hired by a man named Tsong Park who represented the Reverend Moon from Korea who was being indicted for bribing Congressmen to get foreign trading contracts for Korea. Many Congressmen received large cash payments called "gifts of the heart" for cooperating. One of Mr. Park's associates and liaisons to important people was one of, if not my number-one opponent and adversary at the academy, the "honorary alumnus", Milt Nottingham, who was closely associated with Mr. Robert Blackwell, the maritime administrator who terminated me. Hundly said the S.O.B. Nottingham who had cooperated with Park and made money by connecting him with the right people and opened up dummy corporations for him had turned government witness against his client Park. At the same time, Mr. Robert Blackwell, who refused to give me tenure, was under scrutiny by a Queens Congressman concerning a sweetheart deal with major shipping companies. Everything seemed to be breaking my way. Eventually, the *Philadelphia Inquirer* did a major exposé of the entire impropriety.

In 1976, Penn State added Miami to its schedule in place of the University of Maryland, making the schedule one of the toughest in the country. Also, the Penn State team was relatively young. The new, powerful intersectional schedule along with our TV highlight show not only would disarm skeptics but would improve national recruiting. There was one major hitch. Although the show was considered first class by the viewers and critics, Goldberg was having trouble selling it to a network in the northeast that was willing to give Penn State a good time spot. Regardless of the quality of any TV presentation, to maximize the graphic benefits, a good time slot is essential. For example, if the show were viewed at 1:00 a.m. it would have few viewers. Mr. Goldberg and Joe tried everything to no avail. One day, Goldberg told me he had been in New York trying to make a deal with WOR-Channel 9, but was turned down. I told him I had an old Brooklyn friend, Jim Reardon, who knew the president of that network, maybe I could help? Nelson said, "Go ahead".

Jim Reardon was a well-known man in New York City. He had some problems with the law when he was on the police department, and my father tried to help him. The Reardons were former neighbors in Brooklyn and I hung out with Jim's younger brother Bill. At one time, Jim had his own restaurant and bar in mid-Manhattan, called the "Cafe James". He also had a meat business. If you wanted to get something done, and he liked you, he had the right contacts.

In street jargon, it is known as giving a guy a contract. If you had helped him in the past he owed you and would try his best on your behalf. Jim spoke to his pal Don O'Neal, a fellow I had met with Jim at a few sports events. Don was a talented, smart Irishman and boss of WOR. Not only did we get a time slot for $10,000 per show, we were scheduled in the 8:00 p.m. on Monday nights, right before the Monday Night Pro Football game.

Many a sport emporium in New York that would be crowded with advertisement and media people would watch our show while waiting for the pro football game to come on. Most important, Channel 9 encompassed the entire northeast area and beyond. Nelson and Joe were ecstatic. The show was well received and many great players who went to Penn State came because Penn State was brought into their living rooms. After we accomplished that goal, everyone attached to and associated with the show began to take credit. The fact is, it was Joe's idea, Nelson's money, and unbeknownst to Joe, it was my friend Reardon who got the job done. As my old friend Jake Lamotta used to say, "How soon they forget".

Joe was getting closer and closer to achieving his dream of the "Grand Experiment". The '76 record was only 7-5, with a loss to Notre Dame in the Gator Bowl, but the trained eye could see a major breakthrough was coming in the near future.

In the middle of the season, I received notice that I unanimously won my appeal and was reinstated as an associate professor at the academy. Mr. Blackwell resigned his position. Tsong Park was forced to leave the country (Hundly saved him from jail) and a nosey reporter from the *Philadelphia Inquirer* concluded that something was rotten at the academy. Her curiosity was predicated on why a big government bureaucrat like Blackwell cared about my getting tenure. Being a political reporter, she got the okay from her editor and what a job she did. I, the academy and others were on the front pages of the *Philadelphia Inquirer* for a week.

Technically I could have reclaimed my job as head football coach, but not knowing the outcome of my case, the school had gone out and hired a new coach. His name was Clive Rush. Rush had been a former assistant coach with the New York Jets when they won the Super Bowl. But poor Clive had a drinking problem and was considered emotionally unstable. Because the team rebelled, a scandal broke in *Newsday* citing the players' complaints and some bizarre personal conduct by Rush. Clive was fired one year after he was hired. But I had made up my mind, I was finished coaching, especially at the academy. The only thing that would interest me would have been an assistant's job in the pros, if Joe decided to take that route. So now I had become an associate professor in the department of physical education. Needless to say, I was persona non grata. My victory and the subsequent events had put the academy in a bad light. So I was allowed to do my job and was left alone for the time being. Being part of Penn State was fun and one big-time coach in the family was enough. Some of Joe's enemies would shudder to think there were two of us to contend with.

# Chapter Thirteen

# THE BIG PUSH

Two of Joe Paterno's heroes are Winston Churchill and General George Scott Patton. Their forte was meticulous planning down to the last detail. And if victory was to be achieved, strategic planning might have to be circumvented at specific times to gain the objectives. In military terms, when the time was right, you made the big push. Unfortunately, in times of war, lives are lost. Joe's plans would emulate his two heroes in his endeavor, and though lives might not be lost, possibly some friends would be. Joe had planned for his big push to break out to give him a chance to achieve the "Holy Grail", a national championship.

When TV began focusing on sports, a great deal of money was to be made. The middle class and below, mostly blue collar groups, were doing pretty well financially, due to the unions. They were making enough money to buy houses, raise families and buy a few drinks at the local tavern. More important, the TV moguls knew that suddenly a great portion of America's working force had more free time than ever before. They were bored. What better way to transfer that boredom into big money for the TV networks? The antidote for boredom was sports, a most insidious narcotic. After all, the average man

was too busy raising a family and didn't have time to participate and gain the fame and fortune that would come through
sports enterprises. Although it was only a vicarious participa-
tion, the American male threw himself into this new narcotic
of TV sports.

Guys like Roone Arledge from ABC, Barry Frank for CBS
and others created and emphasized to the top TV moguls the
need and demand for sports by the American male. Boy, did
they ever hit the target and make vast fortunes. Ironically,
most of the producers of big-time sports on TV never wore a
jock strap and probably their worst injury could be covered
with a band-aid. Suddenly the word "sports" now equalled
money.

As the new movement in TV sports began to affect our
society, it reminded me of what Professor Marshall McCluhan
was trying to say. Our society's intellectual perspectives and
balance were being denigrated to the shallow concepts of
sports. Suddenly we had sports commentators who became
surrogate representatives for legendary historical generals,
politicians and moreover, educators. Howard Cosell crowned
himself a genius. A genius of what? Where were his creations
that might change not only our society, but the world? Young
sportswriters, most of them who were aficionados, buffs, and
dilettantes, started to promiscuously bestow compliments of
genius on coaches, writers and media people. When I see a
coach earn and receive a Nobel Prize, I might reconsider my
opinion. Joe Paterno was no genius when he pursued his
goals, but he could be compared to the great military men
and statesmen who planned and had the courage to implement and finally promulgate their achievements. What Joe
Paterno was doing in 1975, 1976, and 1977 was preparing for
the encounters that were to come if he was to prove the
"Grand Experiment" could be achieved.

When a man is on a mission and challenges the concepts of other people's inveterate beliefs, he must expect some
form of retaliation. In 1977, Penn State went 11-1 with a blow-
out victory over a strong Arizona State team in the Fiesta Bowl.
Their national ranking was only number five. 1978 looked

like another potentially great season. Chuck Fusina, the quarterback was one of the best in the country and the two defensive tackles, Bruce Clark and Matt Millen, might have been the best tandem in the land. Both eventually became great professional players. Millen was white and Clark African-American, and they were called the salt and pepper boys.

They intimidated every opponent. Other stars were wide out Scott Fitzke and running back Mike Guman. This team looked like they would give Penn State and Joe Paterno their first true national championship. But once again as in 1976, sick people began to surface before the season started. In '76 and '77, Joe was getting mail threats against himself and his family. Someone had followed one of his daughters home and knew of her daily school routine. Naturally it was upsetting. The FBI was informed and for awhile Joe had to coach with a heavy burden on his mind.

Chuck Fusina, star quarterback, had also received threatening letters concerning himself and his widowed mother. It seemed like a conspiracy to derail Joe and Penn State.

In the '76 Pitt game, an actual threat was made on Joe's life and Fusina's mother's. The game went on, but the FBI were all over the field protecting Joe and Fusina. From 1976 until 1978, the threats came. The FBI concluded it was the same person mailing from different postal zones, but no one was ever caught. Suddenly the threats stopped. He or she, like many others, had been steamrolled by the Penn State express.

After going 11-0 in 1978, Penn State would play a great Alabama team coached by Bear Bryant for the National Championship. The location was the Sugar Bowl. Alabama was the winner of the Southeast Conference and it was rumored every coach in the conference was offering information to Bear Bryant about how to beat Penn State. It was the South, coached by the kingfish of the "good old boys," against the extremely confident, annoying, skinny "wop" leader from the East.

The records show Penn State lost, 14-7. Penn State was stopped three times on the famous goal-line stand that became history. They played well enough to win, but didn't get the brass ring. Alabama became National Champions and Penn State ended up number four. It was so close, Joe knew his dream was achievable in the near future. After all, in 1977 and 1978, Penn State went 22-2. The only two losses were at the hands of Kentucky in 1977 and Alabama in 1978. Everyone could smell a National Championship in the near future.

The big push continued through 1981. Penn State was 28-8, with Bowl wins over Tulane, Ohio State and Southern California. By then, Joe had proved Penn State was big time in every way, but somehow the Holy Grail, the National Championship, continued to elude them.

# Chapter Fourteen

# MOUNT EVEREST

One could feel the electricity going into the 1982 season. Penn State had finished with a 10-2 record and a Bowl victory over Southern Cal in 1981. Again, JoPa was to have a chance to prove that PSU could be number one.

The success of the last four years on the national level had put Joe and the school under the national microscope. Could this team be so good with such a clean program? And was this coach for real? He had been accepted and tolerated as a success from the regional east; now he was threatening the mainstream of major college football. He was cracking the infrastructure of the "good old boys" and he was saying and doing all the right things. Was Joe on the verge of being the dominant voice for big-time football? People across the country began to follow Penn State and Joe Paterno.

Approaching the 1982 season, I was still at the academy. When I had returned and resumed my residence in Port Washington, my sister, whose husband was doing very well, moved to a nice area called Brookville and we brought my mother to an apartment house in Glen Cove. Between Cis and me, once or twice a week we would go and do the shopping for her and not much else changed. We seldom heard from Joe, he was always very busy. But her funds had been running out since my Dad's death. I declared myself head of the household again and between Cissy's and Joe's contributions and my own support, we were able to manage okay. Joe sometimes forgets that every Mother's Day, Easter, Christmas and any other holiday he had the assurance that Mom would not be alone, and I had many good times taking her out, especially on Mother's Day and Easter. She would also go over to Cissy's a lot and babysit as Cissy's family began to grow with three boys.

Back at the academy, Superintendent Admiral Engle had retired. Watergate and Korea Gate had faded away, but Nottingham and a few other alumni still had strong political contacts in Washington. So they were able to get an alumnus the job as Superintendent named Tom King. Reagan had replaced Carter, and King was told to leave me alone. He wasn't a bad guy, a bit of a traditionalist, but part of the maritime bureaucracy. Eventually he would ask me to assume the role of athletic director. King and his wife had class, that's more than I could say for his successors.

After my ordeal at Michigan State and the academy, and my failure at finding the right woman, I was content to be a free spirit who wouldn't be corrupted by the unseemly dictates of our materialistic society. After all, I was over 40 and content to be who I was. Churchill had said, "You aren't a complete person unless you can entertain people, be entertained by people and entertain yourself." Then I met Barbara.

As a young man at home when Dad was alive, I used to watch the Bob and Ray Comedy Show on TV. I was familiar with them. When Joe and I attended Brown, Bob and Ray were the hottest radio show in the nation. They were hilarious with their dry, clean, brilliant humor. If there are such things as comedic geniuses, Bob and Ray would have to be included. Dad loved them, it was his favorite show. Never did I dream I would be involved with Ray Goulding's daughter, Barbara, and get to know all the Gouldings.

One summer day in the second year of my return to the Academy, I went to the local pharmacist in Great Neck. Working behind the counter doing book work was this tall girl with beautiful long, black hair. Her features were exquisite, but she had the saddest brown eyes, like those of a lost doe in the forest. She looked about 23 or 25 at that time. I felt a spark for the first time in a long time, but I thought she was too young, so I kept my distance.

Much to my surprise, on my next visit, the owner of the pharmacy asked to speak to me. The girl was not there. The owner proceeded to tell me who she was and what a wonderful person she was. The owner was married with daughters of his own so I knew he was sincere. He told me she was interested in meeting me and gave me her telephone number. I had ambivalent feelings about calling her, but felt one date couldn't hurt.

We went to a nice Italian restaurant and after a good meal, we talked for hours. She was extremely bright, had a great sense of humor but was really mixed up. She was living at home with her parents and her sister. There were six Gouldings and Barbara was the first girl. Her father doted on her and she became his favorite. As a child she emulated everything he did, including his eating habits. Ray Goulding was a big man, about six foot three, who enjoyed eating. He weighed about 230 pounds. Before reaching the trying age of female adolescence, Barbara was exceedingly overweight. Her mother, "Liz", a tall, thin woman, didn't want her daughter carrying the burden of obesity, so she constantly scolded Barbara about her weight. That created a personality conflict that was in existence when I met her. Her adoring father had been the true culprit, but by the time she was 18 years old, Barbara was five foot eight and 190 pounds. When I met her at the age of 23, she had slimmed down to 123 and actually wore clothes well enough to be a model. But the damage had been done, she could only see herself in the mirror as a fat, ugly girl.

Having gone through a similar period in my teens, not only did I sympathize with her, but I was full of compassion. From that day until the day she passed away in 1994 from multiple sclerosis, I tried to convince her she was beautiful. Whether her temporary anorexia had anything to do with her getting MS, I don't know. Barbara was another sensitive young lady, highly intelligent, caught up in a changing time for females. Females who were brought up according to old family values. Barbara could ride horses, write, paint and do all the things that well-bred girls were supposed to do. But her peers were pulling her into different directions. Her inferiority complex made her a mark for people to abuse. This cultured human being whose sensitivity to people, animals, flowers and everything in nature may have been too refined to survive the callous society we live in. By far, Barbara was the best liked of all the women I brought to Joe's home. Diana and Mary Kay, Joe's daughters, were especially fond of her.

After a few dates, I met Mr. Goulding, who was as big as life. He told me he used to go to the Academy to watch our games. He was also a big fan of Joe Paterno and Penn State. He knew how old I was, but he knew I treated his daughter properly. Barbara and I kept company on and off for about seven years. Like the women I had known, she wasn't sure if she wanted to get married. At least I instilled in her some confidence.

A couple of months after we met, she left the pharmacy and went to work for a big drug company called Scheins of Roslyn, N.Y. Within two years, she became an executive, and the boss's son wanted to marry her. She said no, and just when she began to find a comfortable niche in life, she became ill. Barbara died at the age of 41 after suffering for six years. Never have I felt such remorse and despair. But at least I knew she got to see Penn State win its first National Championship in 1982. She went home on the plane carrying an empty magnum of champagne and wearing a cowboy hat. She said it was the best time she ever had.

My interest in football and meditation helped me through this difficult time. Contrary to what people think, I never was a womanizer. I was merely fortunate enough to know more than one lovely person. Too often we stereotype people who are different and live differently without knowing the true facts.

Going into the 1982 season, Joe had a good nucleus back from the 1981 squad that was 10-2 with a win over Southern Cal in the Fiesta Bowl. The big difference was stability at the quarterback position. Penn State usually had a strong running game, and 1982 would not be any different. Curt Warner and Herschel Walker from the University of Georgia, Penn State's opponent, were two of the best running backs in the country. But a big serious kid (whose dad was a coach), Todd Blackledge, would give Penn State a superb passing game to complement its running game. Penn State and Joe always tried for balance on offense, but sometimes the passing was weak and Penn State thrived on the run.

Joe had begun to get a reputation for being overly conservative on offense. Not in 1982; taking advantage of Blackledge and a fine receiving core of Garrity, Fitzke, McCloskey, and Warner coming out of the backfield, Penn State would compile more yardage passing than running. The 1982 Sugar Bowl was a dream game. Georgia, led by Heisman trophy winner Herschel Walker was ranked number one. Penn State came in ranked number two. Georgia had the best secondary in the nation and they were challenged by a potent Penn State passing game. The hype for the game was unbelievable. Joe would again have his chance to compete with the elite; I guess he didn't learn his lesson against Alabama. If the word "rednecks" is indigenous to the south it would be endemic to the State of Georgia. They came to the game in great numbers and Penn State brought an unexpected amount of fans. The City of New Orleans was in a state of revelry for a week before the game.

Dave Hartman, from ABC's morning show was there, and I was assigned to get him and Joe's family to the game. Surely this would be one of the greatest of all Sugar Bowls.

Georgia and Herschel Walker had run roughshod over all their opponents. Walker was truly a fantastic back, six-foot-two, 225 pounds, with a sprinter's speed; he was an unselfish, dedicated player—truly a force. But Penn State had a history of stopping Heisman trophy winners: Terry Baker from Oregon State (Gator Bowl), Marcus Allen in the Fiesta Bowl—could they stop Herschel Walker? This time Penn State had to fish or cut bait. The National Championship, the Holy Grail, the Grand Experiment, Don Quixote had another chance to get to the highest peak and eliminate all doubt.

Penn State won the toss and chose to receive. The return team brought the ball back slightly past their 20. And much to the fans' surprise, Blackledge hit the tight end McCloskey on the first play for first down. Then he hit him again, splitting double coverage for a long gainer and another first down. Two plays and two passes and two first downs. After the third consecutive pass and first down, Penn State's fans roared. Joe Paterno was successfully attacking Georgia at its defensive strength. Rest assured this Penn State team had come to play. After a fourth consecutive completion, the ball was given to Curt Warner on a draw play and another first down. Before Georgia knew what hit them, a couple plays later, Warner bounced outside to the left and went in for the first score. It looked so easy. But did Penn State score too quickly? Nobody had come close to stopping Herschel Walker and the Georgia offense all year long.

As expected, Georgia lined up in a pro "I", and the first play was a pitch to Walker to the right side for a short gain. Georgia went three downs and out and once again Penn State had the ball and was on the move. From the first play, Penn State was in control of the game. The final score was 27-23, but with about six minutes left in the game, Kevin Baugh, who had a great game returning punts and kick-offs, got reckless. Georgia had punted deep into Penn State's territory. The smart play would have been with the game winding down, to go for a safe "fair catch". Penn State was leading 27-17, and Georgia needed two scores to beat them. Baugh disdained the fair catch and tried to run it back and fumbled. This was the break Georgia was looking for. Their fans went wild. When Georgia scored on a trick quarterback roll out right throw back left (someone had failed to cover a tight end coming across the field against the grain) I got a sick feeling in my stomach. Was this going to be another Alabama disappointment?

If Penn State lost, the press and alumni would have a feast on Joe's bones. Now the score was 27-23. Georgia went for two and the score remained 27-23. Only a touchdown would now beat Penn State. After the kick off return, Penn State went to a two-tight end offense with Curt Warner and Jonathan Williams pounding the ball inside and taking time off the clock. Adding a clutch third-down completion, Penn State would run the clock out and win its first National Championship. JoPa (his new nickname) had given the fans what they wanted. He completed his "Grand Experiment" and now sat atop his Mount Everest.

And anybody who doesn't believe he meticulously planned and orchestrated the 1982 season, doesn't know Byzantine Joe. From now on he would get the respect he deserved. Joe, like Sinatra, was becoming "The Chairman of the Board". If he had run for the Governor of Pennsylvania he would have won. Where would he go from here? For the Don Quixote of football, the impossible dream came true. What quest was he planning for the future?

# Chapter Fifteen

# JOE THE MORALIST

A fter the unbelievable success in 1982, Joe was developing a glorified image in his fans' eyes. Before 1982, Joe was a well-known, visible football coach, but after '82 he became a genuine celebrity. He wasn't a cult figure, but he was a hero to the blue-collar fan, and of course, to all Penn State alumni.

Joe and Sue had always been interested in politics, maybe Sue more so than Joe. I think she may have envisioned herself as the governor's wife. After the revelry and the celebration was over, Joe was back to the grindstone. But I saw there was a change, he really was considering big-time politics and he was planning and maneuvering in that direction. Joe was leaving his options open. He had achieved a gigantic victory. But he surely wasn't the first coach to win a National Championship. And Bear Bryant had more Bowl victories. And no one had won all the major Bowls. So his next decision would be politics or more football.

One thing that was noticeably visible was the type of people that Joe began to associate with. After every home game, Joe and Sue invited people to what has become known as "Dinner at Paterno's". Each dinner would have different groups, associates, friends, prestigious alumni, and media people, a truly mixed bag. From 1982 on, the dinners became a bit more formal (the food was the same), but the quality of the wine improved, and the guests were more from a political milieu. The faces at the table were now the Board of Trustees, the most prestigious and rich alumni, fund raisers and the most elite of the administration. All the guests had an assemblance of a group who were performing as a political committee to get someone elected.

Joe's political ties became more visible, and with the Republicans ensconced in Washington, he openly backed Republicans in state elections. He became a close friend of the late and prestigious revered Senator John Heinz, also Arlen Specter, and many Congressmen and the major fund raisers for the party. Joe and Sue seemed to be planning a possible lateral move to politics. Maybe it was a realization of not being a millionaire himself, being an Italian Catholic or thinking of failures of other public sports figures who ran for office, but whatever it was, he changed his mind and concentrated on protecting and solidifying what he achieved for football. Joe's political views are too transitory for him to have been an apparatchik type of politician.

I think the reasons Joe and Sue seriously considered getting into the political arena were that they felt they could influence the morals of young people caught up in a convoluted changing society. The family structure in the country was deteriorating and young people were being inundated with drugs and promiscuous sex. Maybe a sports icon could have a positive effect. Instead of the sports forum, maybe Joe could send his message through the political forum. But I'm happy he changed his mind and stayed in football.

Is Joe Paterno a hypocrite? His enemies would love to prove that accusation. Complex men are difficult to definitively categorize intellectually.

Hypocrites are people who espouse certain idealistic values and moral principles while at the same time they knowingly violate and contradict them. Joe Paterno may change his mind concerning key issues, but that's not hypocrisy, that's capriciousness.

Yes, Joe Paterno can be a capricious person. People who know and respect Joe, enemies and friends, all agree that as a coach he has no peer. Maybe he's the best ever. But when he begins to pontificate, he sometimes offends people, including some of his admirers. Joe and Sue are so intensely focused on their family and how they live and what they believe in, that sometimes they forget there are many unfortunate people, who for a million different reasons haven't had their good fortune. Happiness is not always tethered to self-discipline and morality. But that doesn't make them bad, just different.

Although Joe and Sue are English majors (constantly correcting people who use bad grammar) and admire the arts, I doubt if history's most controversial classic writers and painters would be invited to dinner. Writers like Balzac, Voltaire, Capote, Hemmingway, and painters like Michaelangelo, Van Gogh, El Greco, and Modiglananni would not mix too well with Joe's guests. Their societal attitudes would be drastically different. However, as different as they were, you can't say they were bad, and certainly they left their imprint on civilization. Their greatest sin would be they lived counter to the moral standards that existed while they worked. Conversely, their eventual greatness was based on the fact they challenged the society who made the rules.

Once Joe Paterno decided he was going to stay at Penn State for life, he knew he couldn't live on past achievements. Sure, he completed the "Grand Experiment" and sure, he won a National Championship, and sure, he was considered one of the top coaches in the country; probably the successor to Bear Bryant's crown. But if he were to maintain his stature and keep the ear of the media and the public, there could be no let down. As soon as you become "King of the Hill," someone will try to knock you off. With expanded TV coverage, and the financial rewards that were available, more and more schools began to improve their programs. In the next ten years, we would see more quality teams and more parity than in the entire history of college football.

Compared to most teams that win National Championships, Penn State reacted with humility and enjoyed the redolent smell of success. But I sensed a closing of the ranks at the highest level. A palace guard started to form around Joe and his program. And there was the beginning of small petty skirmishing concerning authority, budgetary allotments, and media policy at the administrative level. Not yet serious, but maybe a crack in the structure that bared watching. What Joe and his fans wanted was another National Championship. Notre Dame had been added to the schedule in 1981 and would remain on it until 1992. And often the National Championship went through the Fighting Irish. Joe knew that his adversaries would make Penn State their number-one priority, now more than ever.

Joe got tougher on himself, his staff, and anyone close to the program. You were either with Joe or against him. He no longer was the farcical knight Don Quixote; his new sobriquet was JoPa. There were to be no more dreams. JoPa wanted to be the number-one man in college football. Get with him or get out of his way.

# Chapter Sixteen

# JoPa

I t took Joe and Penn State 16 years to get to the top and he wasn't about to wait another 16. Up to 1982, every incoming group Penn State recruited either went undefeated or played for a National Championship. Could this unbelievable achievement be continued playing against the best teams in the country and many teams with improved programs? There were books being written about Joe. Cardboard cutouts. They even named an ice cream called "Peachy Paterno" after him.

I was happy to be part of the Penn State program. The coach was my brother, but I still felt a bit like an outsider. My role doing TV and some radio was fun, but I was left alone. Sometimes he had to get annoyed at some of my comments but he always had the chalk last (a coaching idiom). So often I became the brunt of his sarcastic humor. I'm not sure his wife Sue and her family appreciated my criticisms, especially if I proved to be correct. But the give and take was in good taste and was actually fun.

Joe's family was beginning to grow up. His two daughters, Diana and Mary Kay (I am prejudiced), were blossoming into beautiful young ladies. I joked that God in his infinite wisdom and kindness gave the girls their mother's looks and not Joe's. And the boys were real boys. Joe has three sons, David; Joe Jr., called Jay; and George Scott, called Scotty. David, the oldest, had survived a serious accident in 1977, causing Joe to miss the only game in his career. Jay is Joe's second oldest son, and George Scott is the baby of the family.

From that point on, my job was to watch his backside and to help if I could. It didn't mean I would not let him know when I thought he was wrong. Especially concerning Brother, now Father Tom Birmingham.

After our fellow student at Brooklyn Prep, William Blatty, wrote *The Exorcist* in 1972, and Father Tom had played a role in the movie, I had arranged for Joe and Sue to meet Father Birmingham who was then in Rome. Joe and Sue were taking one of their very infrequent vacations. I had been to Rome twice, and I thought Father Birmingham would be helpful and show them the real Rome, not the touristic baloney. Of course, by that time the book *The Exorcist* and the movie were an international success. Father Tom was very much in demand, but he made time to meet Joe and Sue in Rome.

For Father Birmingham to meet another of his prize pupils so successful in the sports world kind of balanced Blatty's Hollywood persona and would only display the great intellectual propensities of the Jesuits. When the movie was being filmed in Georgetown, Washington, and New York, on several occasions I accompanied Father Tom to the locations and even a Christmas party. They made Max Von Snydow who played Fr. Merrin, the lead, look like Father Birmingham. Gaunt features, wide mystical eyes and widowed peak crop of gray hair long in the back.

Father Tom, who was so involved in the production that became an artistic and financial success, let his hair grow a bit longer. After Joe's vacation, I asked him and Sue if they enjoyed Rome with Father Birmingham. Joe said it was okay, but Sue didn't feel it was appropriate that this priest who had celebrity status should kiss women when greeting them and let his hair grow long, and Joe agreed. I told them they were being ridiculous and Father Tom was only human and kissing a woman on the cheek certainly was only platonic. But that's how puritanical they had become. I remembered my history. Once Martin Luther made the break from the Church of Rome and the Protestant sects established themselves, in an attempt to outdo Rome they implemented stricter rules of morality for the family and their followers. Although Sue and her Mom are baptized Catholics, many of her relatives were strict Protestants. Maybe Sue and Joe were competing with that side of the family. Both Joe and Sue are devout and conservative Christians.

On another occasion, an alumnus and friend lost favor when he divorced his wife and was seen with a younger woman. Hypocrisy? Answer, No. Capriciousness? Yes. Moralist? Yes. Later on, Father Tom and the alumnus returned to the fold and were back in favor. As Joe was confronted with problems with his team and his now growing children, he had a better understanding of the changing times and realized everyone couldn't be like him. Little by little, his moralism abated and his new image as a flexible, understanding JoPa gained strength.

Things remained the same with my mother. She still was in Glen Cove in New York, and Cissy and I took care of her needs and made sure she had company on the holidays. She saw very little of Joe, her pride and joy, but constantly bragged about his achievements. At times, she even introduced herself as Joe Paterno's mother. And I was beginning to really respect the way she was handling herself living alone. Once she realized this was to be her way of life, she became fiercely independent. All her brothers and sisters were gone, so she accepted the inevitable with dignity. She knew Cissy and I were nearby, and Joe was busy making her famous.

As for myself, I still had a rocky relationship with Barbara Goulding. And between my position at the Academy and my position at TCS, I was making good money but was a bit bored. So when the new superintendent Admiral Thomas King asked me to take over as Athletic Director (on an acting basis) to revitalize the football program and all sports, I said yes. I knew it was a political move and he wanted to better use my talents. My acceptance was based on my being allowed to continue the TV and radio during the football season and would not attend the King's Point games. Frank Broyles, the

Athletic Director of Arkansas, was then the color analyst for ABC, so I easily won my point.

Before I became part of the Penn State media group, being Joe's brother was tough. But now, not only was I still mistaken for Joe in Pennsylvania, but people began to recognize me from the TV show. There were few places that I could go without being approached.

One time with Guido D'Elia, the talented producer of our TV show, I was surrounded by a hostile crowd in a place called Froggy's. Froggy's is in the downtown Pittsburgh area and is a favorite hangout of Pitt fans and I was in there the week before a  big Penn State contest. It was all in fun and we had a good time. But for a while I was sweating. It was then I thought about asking for a raise.

My worst encounter was with the Notre Dame fans. For some reason, Penn State had been very successful against Notre Dame. Not only were there Notre Dame fans all over the East who recognized me, but some, usually the subway alumni type, can be quite arrogant and vociferous. Once in a while it's good to be ugly, because people feel they can't do any more damage to you, so I escaped unscathed. You could tell they resented Penn State's transgressions on Notre Dame's reputation as the most popular team in the East, but you also felt they had deep respect for Joe and the school.

Something I must explain is that being a bachelor, I eat out a lot. Consequently, I go to a lot of restaurants, and of course, restaurants have bars. Maybe in another book I will record my favorite stories from these experiences. When people would ask me if my affiliation with Penn State was based on nepotism, my reply was President John Kennedy appointed his brother Bobby to be the Attorney General. But many people forgot that I had established my own career before Joe's. To be related to a famous person makes one a target. So far, Joe's children are handling it fine.

In 1983, Penn State slipped to 8-4 and one tie with a minor Bowl victory over the University of Washington. Most of the superstars from the 1982 squad had graduated. So Joe had to reload if he was to play for another National Championship. Being the number-one team in the country helps in recruiting and Penn State took full advantage. Many fine players arrived but they were a couple of years away from stardom.

In 1984, things got worse, and Penn State slipped to 6-5, got clobbered by Notre Dame, 44-7, and lost to arch rival Pitt, 31-11, and didn't go to a major Bowl. The boo-birds were back, and as my friend Jake Lamotta said again, "How soon they forget." Some fans had begun to say Joe had become too conservative. But Joe always tries to get the most out of the players he has to use. His quarterbacks, Doug Strang and John Shaffer, were smart but didn't have great arms. However, they worked well within the system and made a lot of those critical third-down completions. So Joe used a short passing game. He also had another great running back in D.J. Dozier and a formidable line, so they ran the ball. This was not the offense of 1982. The heart of the team was an improving strong defense and specialty teams, mostly all coming back for the next year, so he was thinking ahead to '85 and '86.

In 1985, John Shaffer brought stability to the quarterback position, the defense was assuming the stature of 1982, and Joe Paterno's formula for success once again was working. Decisive victories over Alabama, Notre Dame, and Pitt put Penn State into the Orange Bowl against a strong Oklahoma team with another National Championship on the line.

In a tough football game, Penn State lost to Oklahoma, 25-10, and finished third in the national ranking. It was then Joe became friendly with coach Barry Switzer from Oklahoma. Joe changed his opinion of Switzer, once again showing his ability to be flexible in his attitude toward people. He still didn't approve of what Barry had done and had been associated with in previous years at Oklahoma. But after learning about Barry's childhood and background, he showed compassion and hoped to have a positive influence on Switzer.

Eventually the same thing happened in his relationship with Johnny Majors. Joe did less prejudging and extrapolating. Whether it was another calculated move by Byzantine Joe or not, fellow coaches found him less pompous and righteous. From 1982 on, Joe Paterno and Penn State had begun a bit of a seesaw battle with the media. It seemed the new palace guard with Joe's approval had tightened all access to him, the team, and the Penn State program. The news media were especially resentful and quite upset.

Prior to the 1984 season, our family had to make a difficult decision. Although Mom was in relatively good health for an 86-year-old woman, there were a few incidents that caused worry. Once she burned herself on the electric stove, and another time she let the water run overnight in the bathroom and it seeped through the floor to a room below. A kindly doctor below complained, and said there was no damage, but there could have been if some of the x-ray equipment hadn't been moved. She also fell down and injured her hip. It became apparent that she shouldn't be alone.

When I discussed the situation with Joe, he said he knew of a nursing home in Pennsylvania, but Cissy and I weren't too sure. We knew Mom didn't want to go to a nursing home. We conspired to go to a nice restaurant for lunch to discuss the situation. I picked Mom up and met Cissy and Joe, who had flown in for the meeting. Cissy's husband Phil was also there. Up to that time, Joe had been extremely involved with his job and raising his own family. Feeling Mom needed help and being established personally and financially, he intervened. At first, I resented him taking over, but he was the oldest and he was going to handle all the expenses, and in my heart, I knew in the long run it was the right decision. But it wasn't going to be easy.

At lunch we just had some fun and Joe was running the show. Of course, Mom was happy to be lunching with her famous son. As he does often, Joe was carefully leading up to why we were together.

Then he said to Mom, "How would you like to live in a home in Pennsylvania?" Florence Paterno's demeanor abruptly changed; her big green eyes darted back and forth between my sister and me as if we had betrayed her. We must have talked Joe into springing this trap upon her. Then she began to cry. Joe began to almost recruit Mom into going, explaining it was a beautiful place in the country and how she would be around nice people her own age and mentioned some of the activities. Joe said, "Mom, please give it a try." Joe returned to Pennsylvania to make the arrangements. Cissy and Phil went home and I took Mom to her place. She asked me a lot of questions and I just tried to reinforce what Joe had said. Deep inside I had my doubts.

The date was set for her to go about three weeks after the luncheon. Cissy packed Mom's things and she and Phil were to meet me and Mom at the location. Joe would arrive from Penn State. Joe was right, it was a beautiful place, but it was isolated in the mountains of central Pennsylvania. It would be a five-hour drive each way for Cissy and me to visit and about three hours each way for Joe to visit. And with his schedule, his chances of getting there were slim.

The arrangements had been made; we met all the owners and the administrative staff. We saw Mom's room and the facilities and Cissy unpacked Mom's things. Joe said he had to go. Up till then Mom was okay, but then she began to cry, pleading with us not to leave her there; Joe offered a few more words of consolation and then left, leaving Cissy and me alone with Mom. Deep down inside, Joe is a softy. He didn't want to have to make that final good-bye and walk away knowing Mom wanted him to stay. Believe me, it was tough to finally leave her alone with strangers. It's then you realize the strength of the emotional umbilical cord that is never really cut. We left her crying and reminded her she promised Joe she would give it a try for a couple of weeks. Later on, Cissy and I chuckled over Joe's strategic departure.

It eventually turned out to be the right decision; only after Mom caused some trouble and we pointed out to Joe the place was too remote. Fortunately, Joe found a place in State College a short distance from his home, where he, Sue, and some of the kids could conveniently make visits. While she was in the home, as I expected, Sue visited Mom a lot more than Joe did. My mother remained there until 1989 when she died. I felt good that she and Sue actually became friends. After all, for years they had to share Joe.

Some of the writers who were Joe's biggest supporters felt disillusioned and some of Joe's old close friends seemed to be culled to see if they still belonged to JoPa's new society. But the expectations of the 1986 season and for all the old loyalties, Joe was given the benefit of the doubt. In the past, he always seemed to be doing the right thing.

On paper in 1986, Penn State again looked formidable and a possible top team. It would be a milestone year for Penn State; its 100th football anniversary. Dinners had been arranged in Pittsburgh, Harrisburg and Philadelphia, strong bastions of Penn State alumni. My partner, Stan Savarin, a prominent Pittsburgh media personality, and I, were to be co-emcees. Bob Hope was to speak at each dinner, scheduled three days apart. This was big-time stuff. Everyone who was anyone in the state would be in attendance. It looked like JoPa had another great plan for the Lions' 100th anniversary.

The defense was experienced, tough, and coached by Jerry Sandusky, for years one of the top defensive coordinators in football. Specialty teams, as always, were solid. And the offense would be potent if not explosive. John Shaffer had become an established quarterback who wouldn't have Heisman statistics, but was a born winner. He was in many ways a superior clone of Joe Paterno as a college quarterback. This would be a later version of the '68, '69 teams. Defense would dominate.

Led by D.J. Dozier, Shaffer, and a big fullback by the name of Steve Smith on offense and Shane Collins, Bob White and a bevy of fine linebackers on defense, the 1986 team had 11 wins and no defeats. Again, a natural matchup for the National Championship was a possibility. Number two Penn State versus Miami in the Fiesta Bowl. Being independents not tied into conferences allowed each school to go head to head to the benefit of the host Fiesta Bowl.

Miami had a super squad led by Heisman Trophy winner Vinny Testaverde and wide receiver Michael Irvin and a host of great offensive players. The defense was just as good, led by one of college's all-time great defensive tackles, the late Roger Brown, Cortez Kennedy, and also a host of great linebackers, like Stubbs and Armstead. It looked like a mismatch. The '86 Miami team had 21 players who were eventually drafted by the NFL. Penn State shouldn't even show up!

JoPa, now respected as a dangerous, accomplished warrior, had to have a plan. This was football's Armageddon. The lily white Penn State program with no-frill uniforms, with their moralistic, monolithic conservative coach who always wore a tie, against the hip and the almost funky Miami coach Jimmy Johnson, with his cemented hairspray coiffure. Johnson was the leader of the "wild bunch" of college football. The irreverent, undisciplined anti-everythings the sport was all about; men who wore combat fatigues when they traveled. Was it the good versus the bad? JoPa and his wonderful assistants contrived the master plan. A plan that would emphasize brains over brawn. Even Joe knew Miami had better athletes but not better people, and in the toughest of battles, it's the better people with the most character who generally win.

To kill a great snake, one must first cut the head off. Likewise, to neutralize great organizations, it's best to eliminate the top man. Joe knew the fantastically talented Miami pro offense was triggered by the quarterback Vinny Testaverde. A big six-foot-five, 225-pound kid; not only was he a great passer, but he could bounce off pursuing defenders and still make the big play. Miami coach Jimmy Johnson had worked extremely hard teaching Vinny to read conventional defenses. So the first and biggest part of Penn State's game plan would be to neutralize Mr. Testaverde, and to do so he would have to be contained, pressured, but most of all, confused.

In one of the greatest college football games of all time, viewed by one of the largest TV audiences, the jacket and tie good guy, the ultra-square coach beat the unbeatable "mod squad" of super athletes led by their hip "good old boy" coach from Arkansas, 14-10.

If Joe could have won the governorship of Pennsylvania in 1982, he could have done the same thing in Arizona in 1986. Because of the immense importance of the game, I had gone to Scottsdale early to be with Joe and the team. My company, TCS, was showing the game on cable TV.

Practices are always intense, but Joe was really pushing hard. Early each morning he would knock on my door and we would walk miles along the highway and up the beautiful mountains. Everywhere we walked on the highway, people would shout, "Joe get those S.O.B.'s!" People came out of their houses and shouted encouragement. He sure had the locals with him, and when we went to dinner after the victory, fans in the restaurant gave him a standing ovation. So JoPa may not be perfect, but he does represent many things the rank and file of America believe in and respect.

Once again, Penn State had stymied a Heisman Trophy winner. Vinny Testaverde threw five interceptions. Somehow, Byzantine Joe crawled into Testaverde's mind and scrambled his synaptic connections.

A good football team is built on a triangle—defense, offense and special teams. A perfect team would encompass all three aspects in equal proportions. Most teams (many good ones) have an imbalance in one of these categories of the triangular equation. The Penn State '86 squad had a great defense, but would only be rated good in offense and special teams. So in the game plan, the emphasis was on strength, namely defense, and more specifically the defense had to keep the game close enough for the coaches to extract enough from the offense and specialty teams to pull off the upset. And that's exactly what happened.

The defense had five interceptions, the last one by Pete Giftopoulos as Miami was driving for the winning TD. That was fantastic, but earlier, when PSU got the go-ahead and eventually winning TD, the offense made a surprising and rewarding move. PSU needed a TD and was inside Miami's five-yard line. Normally a team will come out in a tight formation to prevent losing yardage by a penetrating defense. To everyone's surprise, especially Miami's, PSU came out in spread out passing formation. It forced Miami to loosen up their defense, but the Lions' TB D.J. Dozier ran the ball wide and got in for the score. A brilliant bit of strategy. That's why Joe got a standing ovation in a restaurant after the game. Again, Byzantine mysticism rose to the occasion.

# Chapter Seventeen

# JOE REPLACES THE BEAR

fter Bear Bryant passed away in 1983, there were a few coaches around ready to assume his role as "Dean" of college coaches. The distinguished Tom Osborne from Nebraska, the personable Bobby Bowden, the wiley Lou Holtz, and of course, Joe Paterno. All were outstanding and all were a credit to football and their respective schools. Although Osborne's win-loss record was outstanding, he had yet to win a National Championship and his record in Bowl Games was dismal, and coach Osborne could be called phlegmatic. Bowden had good success in the Bowls, but he hadn't won a National Championship, and Holtz, always successful, had coached many schools but lacked strong identification to any one of them. So the man who had the complete package, a National Championship, a great record in Bowls, and seniority at one school with a brilliant won-loss record was JoPa. And of course, he always was charismatic and a fine spokesman for major college football.

Joe didn't ordain himself as Bryant's heir, he let the title come to him. But after the second National Championship in 1986, and the cascading awards that followed, there was no doubt who was the new Dean. And I think the Bear would have approved. Although different in a multitude of ways, they were clones in that they loved the sport, were workaholics, and were two of the brightest coaches who ever put on a pair of pants. I would need a total paragraph to list all of Joe's achievements. But in 1986, he was voted his fourth National Coach of the Year by his peers, a record. He was named the first football coach to be picked as "Sportsman of the Year" by *Sports Illustrated* and adorned its cover. Other awards were the Lambert Trophy and Best Coach in the East and a distinguished American Award from the National Football Foundation and many other accolades. Also, Joe hit the big 60.

It was about then the first rumors of his pending retirement surfaced. I didn't know the origin of such rumors that had him leaving Penn State and going into  politics. I knew politics was out, and for retirement, it was none of my business. To say I received 50 calls from various media groups, all wanting to write or to do some documentary on Joe would not be an exaggeration. Joe is not that easy to contact, and with his new palace guard it became even more difficult. To think he would confide in me was an error; Joe confides in no one, except maybe his wife.  His lack of confidentiality vexes some writers, but it's also part of his defense.

I received so many calls I got tired of saying I knew nothing  and got tired of telling everyone what a great guy he was. By 1986 I was along for the ride and was trying to grow old gracefully. But when we were young, Joe and I were called the "Corsican Brothers" because we seemed to be able to read each other's minds. The vibes I was getting were for his desire for another National Championship and more individual records that were obtainable.  But no one knew the Penn State program would come under siege in the near future and face a major setback. And part of the cause was Joe himself. Was he a manipulator or a motivator?

As mentioned, in 1984 there were some minor rumblings and complaints by the writers. They  complained Joe was less and less accessible. And when questioned about matters relating to the team and individual players, they accused him of being evasive and in some cases dishonest. Believe me, Joe is not a guy who won't retaliate if you break a confidence with him. On a few occasions at informal press parties, Joe let his guard down and made comments to the press purportedly off the record and not for print. His trust was violated, and some embarrassing quotes were printed. Consequently, he and his media people tightened security. The many were punished for the indiscretions of a few. At times, some of the writers yelled at me. I tried to explain the cause of the situation. If Joe told them a kid wasn't going to play and he showed up at the game in uniform, it meant he might play. Joe doesn't take kids on trips or dress them if there isn't a chance they might make a contribution.

Some of his oldest writer friends said they felt he manipulated them when they were needed but now he was mistreating them. I answered many questions like that. In fact, more than one writer said Joe should pay me to be his public relations guy. Personally, I thought most of the old writers were great guys, and maybe Joe was on a little bit of a power kick. One scribe wrote an article titled, "Joe Paterno, the Great Manipulator". Many words mean different things at different times. And on many occasions, different words have similar meanings and overlap in their specific interpretations.

By his own admission, Joe manipulates people. Has there ever been any great leader recorded in history who didn't manipulate people? If to manipulate means to influence and shrewdly manage people to make decisions beneficial to oneself or for a cause, then at times we are all guilty to some degree. The key is if the person manipulated is exploited in a damaging way. When a person recruits someone, be it for sports or business, he manipulates. A father will at times manipulate a child. A romantic suitor often tries to manipulate the one he desires. Joe has manipulated many people, including me. The key is to what degree Joe benefited compared to the persons manipulated, and how it fit within the overall philosophy of Joe's notion of "the greater good".

How does manipulation differ from motivation? Semantically speaking, to motivate means to move to action or to impel one, so there is a similarity between manipulating and motivating as there is between complacency and arrogance. The answer lies in the cause, reasons and objective. Like all successful powerful people, at times Joe Paterno has abused his manipulative skills and motivated people for his own self-interest.

The problem with the press grew. And Joe and his associates seemed indifferent. I couldn't help but think about Michigan State and the problems they had after they won their two National Championships. Joe would be too smart to fall into the subtle trap of excessive success. Or would he? Was Joe going the way of the Mexican General Emiliano Zapata, Huey Long, Governor of Louisiana, Richard Nixon, and dozens of leaders throughout history, who once they got to the top forgot how they got there? Not to mention the people who helped them succeed. I intended to watch closely.

Following the '86 season, Joe and Sue also got more involved in activities not directly related to football. They headed fundraising committees for charitable organizations. They got involved in community affairs and at the same time tried to get funds to improve athletic facilities. Joe really was not staying on top of his football program. His opponents were buckling their chin straps to do battle and prevent Joe Paterno and Penn State from steamrolling over all of college football. He was just getting too powerful.

Once again, similar to the aftermath of the first National Championship, squabbling began at the highest level. Most of the issues were petty, concerning who worked the hardest, how money was spent and who spent it. And some of the wives (as they do in big corporations) were sniping at each other. In my opinion, they all had too much to say. But all of the above was a smokescreen. The heart of the matter was Joe wanting to have the final say in some departments not directly under his authority.

Success is like a perfect day and everyone wants some time in the sun. I guess some wives felt their husbands should get more credit. Early on in his career, Joe would have nipped such problems in the bud. Now at times, to get what he wanted he would assume the posture of a tyrant. Was the quicksand of so much success and adulation claiming a new victim? Only the future held the answer.

Going into the 1987 season, JoPa's record of every incoming class being undefeated or playing for a National Championship was still intact. But soon all the variables in the formula didn't seem to properly fit.

Although the '87 team was 8-3 during the season and won a spot in the Citrus Bowl, it didn't play like a Penn State team. They lost to Alabama, 24-13; Syracuse, 48-21; and Pittsburgh, 10-0. The only really good team they beat was Notre Dame, 21-20. Notre Dame went for the two at the end of the game but came up short. Penn State has always played well against Notre Dame. Clemson manhandled Penn State in the Citrus Bowl, 35-10. Not only was it one of the worst coaching jobs that Joe and the Penn State coaches had executed, the team played lethargically and with a lack of intensity. Something was wrong! Was Joe losing touch with his players and coaches? He could be an ogre on the practice field, cutting people down with his effusive, acerbic comments made in that strident monotone voice. 1988 would get much worse.

Penn State's football team hadn't had a losing season since 1938, and Joe never had one; but all that was about to change. On paper, the '88 squad looked pretty good, featuring some fine players like Steve Wisniewski, Andre Collins and Blair Thomas. They won the first two games, beating a good Virginia team coached by George Welsh, a former assistant under Joe and a close friend. Boston College, without the great Doug Flutie, fell short, and Penn State won.

The next game would be Rutgers, coached by another one of Joe's former assistants, Dick Anderson. Anderson and the Rutgers staff outcoached Joe Paterno and his staff and won, 21-16, at State College, Pennsylvania. That loss would be the hole in the dike that would eventually cause the flood that gave Penn State its first losing season in 50 years. It would be the first time that Penn State lost to arch rival West Virginia in eons.

The deciding game that would close the door and would cause Penn State to have its first losing season in 50 years was Notre Dame, and that made the record five wins and six losses. I remember doing the postseason highlights show by a goal post. It was a late fall day and the sky was overcast. The field was festooned with green derbies and green ribbons and they were being blown up and down the field by a cold November wind. My heart was heavy; like other Joe Paterno fans, I didn't believe he would ever have a losing season. Just before I was to go on camera, a beautiful lady came up to me and said, "Don't feel too bad, everyone at Notre Dame really admires Joe Paterno and Penn State." It made me feel better. She had a son on the Notre Dame squad and it was payback time for the Irish. It was the end of what had been an almost unparalleled climb to the top. Was Joe's Odyssey coming to an ignominious end? For two years in a row we only saw a paper imitation of Penn State football. What had gone wrong? What would the future hold? Approaching the 1989 season, all of the fans, as well as the pundits, and those people close to Joe were apprehensive.

Mom was still in the nursing home at State College, but she was fading fast. During her last days, I had more contact with Joe as a brother than in the prior 30 years. Maybe Mom in her own way was aware for the first time since his initial year as coach, Joe Paterno was in trouble. It seemed while my mother was dying, Joe's career had reached its nadir. Emotionally they were that close! Maybe when Mom eventually passed away, Joe reflected and temporarily regenerated himself. I don't know. There were fences to be mended for sure. The press was unhappy and some high school coaches were concerned about which way the program was headed. And some members of the hierarchy were unhappy.

Joe as usual, admitted there were some problems and took the brunt of the fall. If coaches take the credit in good times, then they must take the blame in bad times. Personally, I was hoping he would put a lid on all the female input, including his wife, Sue's. All the kids were grown up, either being in college or graduated and Joe invited Sue to take a more visible role in his work. I'm not sure that was wise. Sue has strong competitive instincts and in defense of her husband she began to criticize people around her, which I think exacerbated a burgeoning internal problem.

As for me? Whether I agreed with him or not, I fully realized how hard he had worked and what he had achieved for our family name. That was most important to me, the name "Paterno", because my father was so unique, so noble and so forgotten. My own ego was nurtured in Joe's success. And in my acceptance as another loyal follower, I didn't want to see him brought down by the parasites and by his own human weaknesses. Sometimes hard work doesn't overcome adversity. Some of the fickle fans thought Joe should retire, after all, he was over 60, and coaching was a young man's profession. Others called him a dinosaur and said that the game had passed him by. Anyone who was really close to Joe knew the criticisms were utter balderdash. Joe realized he needed to regroup and reflect on previous mistakes to get the Penn State express back on track.

Dr. Bryce Jordan, the Penn State president, an old fashioned Texan and a lover of football, had faith in Joe, but he was talking retirement. On many occasions, he and Joe had talked about Penn State getting into a conference. Dr. Jordan had Big Ten contacts so he laid the groundwork for Penn State to eventually be accepted in 1993. But the Big Ten's interest was founded on the premise that a major independent power would add to the conference's prestige and increase attendance.

There was the dire concern of teams in the other conferences all trying to improve quality and get on TV, increase revenues and hope to land in a major Bowl. It was imperative that the dangerous demise of the Penn State football program be brought to an immediate halt. Much would depend on their resurgence to be a top team. Joe was not about to let Dr. Jordan (whom he had great admiration for) down.

And those people, friends and foes who knew Joe intimately would confirm that he was most formidable when he had his back to the wall.

1990 started off poorly, with losses to Texas and Southern California. But the coaches and team hung together, going 9-3 with solid wins over Alabama and Notre Dame. But they lost to a good Florida State team in the first Blockbuster Bowl and failed to make the Top Ten. This was some improvement, but for the first time in Joe's coaching career, the magic number four failed.

The recruits of 1987, at the end of their four-year cycle, were not unbeaten and didn't play for a National Championship. But it was a hell of an improvement over 1989.

Football fans are never satisfied; they seem to want undefeated teams or National Championships every year. Their identification with the team is vicarious and that feeds their ignorance. The most distasteful fans are the ones who never have engaged in competitive sports. And Joe was always a target. Some of the problems of '89 still existed, but Joe seemed to be regaining control.

The 1991 team had outstanding leadership from co-captains Mark D'Onofrio, Keith Goganious and Darren Perry on the defense; and Sam Gash, Al Golden and Terry Smith on the offense. Tony Sacca, who was thrown into the breech as a freshman, was beginning to play quarterback like the great prospect he was. After accepting to meet the 1990 Co-National Championship Georgia Tech in the Kick-Off Classic and winning 34-22, PSU played 13 games, winning 11 and losing two.

Against Georgia Tech, Tony Sacca was red hot as a wide-open Penn State offense totally dominated Georgia Tech. It looked like Byzantine Joe did it again. Penn State was back. What is frustrating to Joe's enemies is that just when you think you've got him down, somehow he bounces back like the Spauldeen ball he used to hit for three sewers (he says) when he was playing stick ball. His mix of hard work and his ledger-domain had stunned his critics. Maybe he shouldn't retire and maybe he wasn't a dinosaur?

Going into 1992, Penn State was still a major independent school. It would have a shot at National Champ Miami at home  with Tony's younger brother John Sacca  at QB and most of the surrounding cast back. There was a chance for a great year. But the internal problems continued to surface. As Joe put one finger in the dike, another hole would surface, and then another. Years ago, there were people to assist in closing these orifices. But there was no help coming. I had an eerie, sick feeling that some of his own people were rooting for him to lose. Maybe he brought it upon himself? He had become aloof, and certainly, like Michigan State did when they won their two championships, had become arrogant. Joe said complacent, I said it looked like arrogance. The press was right, Joe had become supercilious and lost his perspective. The narcotic of success had gotten to him. He talked down to people.

When people have been offended, they have long memories. Some of Joe's early and closest friends were now distant. And after two previous similar occasions, the program still lacked the old harmony. Then came the Miami game. Going into the Miami game, Penn State was 5-0, playing at home but without a big win on national television in a long time. The quarterback was now John Sacca, the brother of Tony.

In 1991, playing Miami at Florida on a hot, humid day, Tony Sacca played the game of his life, but Penn State still lost, 26-20. Miami had lost some good players, and now Penn State had the home field advantage. With a 5-0 record, Penn State was given a good chance to beat Miami. But it wasn't to be. In another close game, State lost, 17-14. No disgrace, Miami was a fine squad. What happened in the second part of the season was an affront to Joe Paterno's pride.

Historically, Penn State would bounce back from tough losses, put matters behind them and go on to better things. In 1982, Penn State was beaten badly by Alabama but came back to win the National Championship. The 1992 squad just folded. They proceeded to lose to Boston College, Brigham Young, and Notre Dame, none of them great teams. Just a 7-4 season, but they got an invite to play a good Stanford team in the Blockbuster Bowl. Again what happened? Richie Anderson would become a pro back. O.J. McDuffie, who had busted most Penn State receiving records was an All-American. John Gerak and Todd Rucci were as good as most offensive linemen in the country. And on defense they had Reggie Givens, Derek Bochna, and Reggie McKenzie, plus the salt-and-pepper tandem of Jackson and Benfatti at defensive tackles.

Rumors were flying at warp speed. Joe was fighting with his coaches, the administration, the press and even his own team. Take your pick. For possibly only the second time in his illustrious career, he seemed to have lost the kids.

There was even talk of a race problem. This was not a happy team getting ready to play an excellent Stanford squad, with new coach Bill Walsh of the San Francisco 49ers and Super Bowl fame at the helm. Walsh had inherited a fine group of athletes recruited by Dennis Green, who left to take the Minnesota Vikings job. So it was a role reversal between Green and Walsh. As everyone in football knows, give Bill Walsh outstanding talent and he would be tough to beat. A victory over Walsh and Stanford could salvage some pride and respect.

The press had a natural format to promote the game, two distinguished successful coaches, one from the pros and one who was the Dean of college coaches. Both had been crowned geniuses at some time in their careers. It was not Penn State vs. Stanford, it was Paterno vs. Walsh. As one writer metaphorically described the matchup, it was Joe (General Patton) vs. Walsh (General Rommel), meaning the smashmouth Lombardi-like coach versus the silky, slick, sleight-of-hand Walsh. It really was an unfair showdown. Walsh had a better team offensively and defensively and Penn State was struggling. To compound matters, a major incident occurred during the prebowl practice.

Reggie McKenzie, one of Penn State's best linebackers, a guy you needed to make some big plays to disrupt the rhythm of the smoothly programmed Stanford offense, didn't show up for practice. Reggie came from Fort Lauderdale and he went home for a visit and, for whatever reason, had missed practice without notifying any of the coaches. At Penn State, that's a super no-no. Although Joe could have faked an excuse he didn't; Reggie McKenzie was told he would not play in the Bowl game.

Reggie McKenzie was a good kid and Joe knew that. He and Sue had done many things to help him develop as a person. But Reggie could be easily misled by his peers from the ghetto and that's probably what happened. Joe refused to accept any excuses. Joe's son Jay, who was Reggie's friend, tried to intervene. Jay had recently been married and Reggie not only was in the wedding party, but spoke from the altar. Jay had been a member of the team and loved Reggie. Joe was implacable and intransigent at the same time. "Reggie can be on the sidelines, but he will not play," said Joe Paterno. Jay demurred and reminded Joe that all of Reggie's friends would be at the game and Reggie was one of the best players ever to come out of the Fort Lauderdale area and it would be his last game for Penn State. Once again, Joe said no.

I too liked McKenzie; I had given him the name of "Batman." This nickname caught on and he enjoyed the moniker. And when Reggie smiled there was a warm feeling all around. So I also would approach Joe using a different tactic. "You know," I said, "Reggie is really liked by the other black players and your decision might cause a negative ripple effect on the team". I also reminded him there was a lack of good vibes on the team since the Miami game. And I couldn't help but think what the press would say if Joe lost. "Genius Walsh Out-Coaches Paterno". That bothered me. My solicitous endeavor went for naught. Joe knew what was at stake, and he said, "I have to worry about future players, so I can't make exceptions". That took guts, because I felt he knew Penn State would probably lose. And he also told me to "mind my own business".

Well, Stanford beat Penn State, 24-3. It was a repeat of the pitiful performance versus Clemson in 1987. After the game, only a few assistant coaches dropped by his suite. I stayed. It was one of Joe's lowest days as a coach. He knew he had lost the kids and maybe other people. The next day the local press, who had criticized and disparaged Joe from the time they knew McKenzie wouldn't play, really assailed him. "Walsh gave Joe a coaching lesson" read the headlines. Little did they know. As much as I respect Walsh, once he lost coach Green's players, he didn't fare too well, and he decided to leave college coaching. In college you can't buy or trade for quality players. Sometimes you have to play with what you have. Come hell or high water.

It's hard to criticize a brother considered much more successful than yourself. Especially when you admire his achievements and appreciate the glory he brought to the family name. But we were always philosophically different. It was hard for me to admit to myself that I had lost some respect for Joe in the way he had acted over the last years. Something I couldn't believe was happening.

Penn State, with all its quality people and ideals were making the exact same mistakes  Michigan State did, staffed with people of opposite beliefs and character. Maybe it was part of the equation of power and success that I had refrained from. "Larry" became my only salvation. What would Larry do? Join the critical ingrates or would he advise me to speak to a brother I admired and tell him something was wrong?

But still, Joe was my brother and Dad's memory was always there. So I decided to assert myself and I wrote a letter. In the letter I wasn't telling the emperor he had no clothes on, but maybe something no longer fitted well. To have impact and not challenge or threaten Joe I had to be discreet. In some manner I had to find a way to let him know what I had sensed, heard and knew. You don't take Joe on head to head, so I used some of his own strategy. I sent a letter to Mr. Frank Giardenia from the sports information department, who ran our radio program. Frank is a great young man hired to handle media affairs. A family man with three kids and he loved Joe. In my letter to Frank, I poured my heart out about all the distasteful matters of the last years and what solutions I thought could help Penn State get back on track. Carbon copies were sent to several administrators and of course Joe.

Much to my surprise, after a few weeks of apprehension, I received a letter from Joe. From the context I could tell it was carefully constructed after much profound thinking. Mea culpa was the tone of his reply.

"I carefully read and evaluated what you said and I concluded you were right". He further wrote that he knew of the problems and he knew how to resolve them. He would again begin at the bottom. I don't know whether Joe's compassionate admission that many of his problems were his fault was true like the old vintage Don Quixote Paterno or it was the contemporary JoPa who thought he had command of the "real politick" approach to leadership. I still don't know. The "real politick" approach he and Sue had used had blown up in their faces and needed revision and mending.

Joe addressed every problem he had. Personally he sought out the old writers that he had offended and made peace after telling his side. The high school coaches in Pennsylvania were next. They were the ones who helped him because they believed in him, and in the past years they had felt they were ignored. They also were individually sought out by Joe. The rumor had pervaded the high school ranks that all was not well at State College and of course Joe's competitors exacerbated those rumors. All of the negative factors were confronted openly and hopefully honestly by JoPa. He humbled himself to all those people who had helped him in the past, and once again said he needed their aid.

Joe seemingly had bared his soul. This was the Joe who won the hearts of the people from Pennsylvania and Penn State. If it was another of his Byzantine moves, it was a master plan. Like waves following the tide, his legions came to attention and would back him. Even if he was possibly insincere, I was committed to following him.

The healing began almost immediately. Joe reached out to all, especially the team. He began intimate sessions with team players—"Java with Joe"—without sacrificing his intrinsic values of discipline. He investigated and considered extraneous factors before making binding decisions. In essence, he ameliorated some of his attitudes, similar to when he adjusted his moralistic persona that had offended many people.

My father, Angelo Lafayette Paterno, served as a strong role model for Joe and me.

An early family photo with Mom, Dad, Cissy, and Cissy's new dog.

Joe and I fishing together at Sheepshead Bay in Brooklyn.

Joe, Mom, Cis and me together at a family cookout.

"The Corsican Brothers" together at a family gathering.

Joe (far right) idolized mentor and Penn State coach Rip Engle (far left) and became his first new assistant coach in 1950.

Joe and Sue with daughters Diana (front) and Mary Kathryn (rear) celebrate Joe's announcement as Penn's State's new coach in 1966.

I was appointed the head coach at the U.S. Merchant Marine Academy one year before Joe took over the helm at Penn State.

Joe and Cleveland Browns quarterback Milt Plum. Milt was the first of many great quarterbacks who played for Joe.

Following the 1970 Orange Bowl victory over Dan Devine's Miami team, everyone (including Joe and son David) was touting Penn State as the number-one team in the country.

I often wondered if Joe would try his hand in politics. Here he is in January of 1973 assuring Governor Milton J. Schapp that he planned to remain PSU's football coach after it was rumored he was considering running for Governor. He received many letters from PSU fans asking him not to leave coaching.

Joe may look discouraged on the sidelines, but he's actually focusing on what his next strategic move should be to lead the Lions to victory.

The Nittany Lions were Cotton Bowl bound for New Year's Day 1972.

Joe and Texas coach Darrell Royal share a pregame laugh before the 1972 Cotton Bowl Game. Penn State won by a score of 30-6.

Joe has starred at many press conferences over the years. At this one in 1972 he announced his intention to stay at PSU instead of joining the New England Patriots.

With Joe the player always comes first. Here he is in 1971 with quarterback John Hufnagel.

Joe is all smiles after defeating LSU in the 1974 Orange Bowl by a score of 16-9.

Joe with 1973 Heisman Trophy winner John Cappelletti. Cappelletti's moving acceptance speech in which he dedicated the trophy to his dying brother didn't leave a dry eye in the house. (Photo courtesy of Penn State University.)

Legendary Buckeye coach Woody Hayes accepts congratulations from Joe after Hayes' team beat the Lions 17-9 in a September 1975 game.

Joe accepts the tenth
Lambert Trophy awarded to
Penn State since he took
over leadership of the
Nittany Lions. All together
PSU has won 23 Lambert
Trophies under Joe's tenure.

*New York Times* sportswriter
Gordon White presents Joe
with the award for the 1983
Eastern Coach of the Year.
Joe has won four National
Coach of the Year awards.

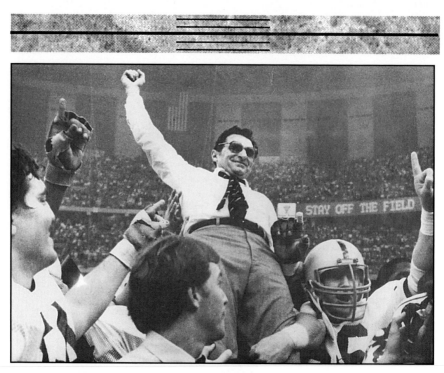

The players show their admiration for Coach Paterno after Penn State's 1983 Sugar Bowl victory and completion of the "Grand Experiment." (Photo courtesy of Penn State University.)

Joe presents a Penn State football jersey to President Ronald Reagan during the 1986 National Champions' White House visit. (Photo courtesy of Penn State University.)

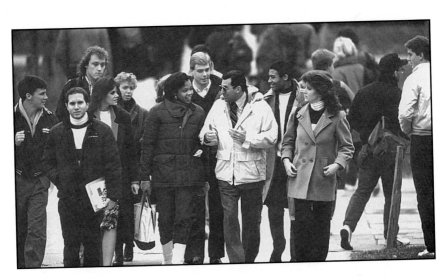

Joe loves to mingle with students and fans at Penn State.
(Photo courtesy of Penn State University.)

Joe always finds time for autographs for Nittany Lions fans.
(Photo courtesy of Penn State University.)

Penn State's Beaver Stadium is a beloved centerpiece of life for Joe and PSU fans and is currently known as the "House that Joe built."

The Nittany Lion is symbolic of Mt. Nittany and Indian folklore and of course, Penn State.

The fans show their support for Penn State's leader at the 1995 Rose Bowl. (Photo courtesy of Penn State University.)

Even during times of leisure Joe is concentrating on the game plan and the win. Here he is poolside working on strategy before the 1997 Fiesta Bowl in Texas.

I have always enjoyed my involvement with Penn State football. Here I am with Bill Zinfer, my former radio partner who is currently the voice of the Miami Dolphins.

Joe and long-time friends at a DKE reunion 45 years after the fact.

Mom and Cissy at Mom's 80th birthday party in Long Island.

Joe, Cissy and I celebrating after a PSU Bowl game victory.

## Joe Paterno: Penn State's Lion King

(Photo courtesy of Penn State University.)

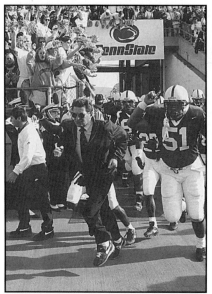

(Photo courtesy of Penn State University.)

(Photo courtesy of Penn State University.)

# Chapter Eighteen

# THE AFRICAN-AMERICAN ATHLETE

B efore African-American athletes began to dominate the game of football, Penn State always had
players who were African-American. Prior to the
integration of schools in the South, no school had an abun-
dance of African-American football players. The African-Americans who became famous in the pros had come from African-
American colleges or were one of a few small groups representing various prestigious white schools. In the late forties
and fifties, when super players like Jimmy Brown, Lenny
Moore, Ollie Mattson, Rosey Grier, and Rosey Brown surfaced
and became great pros, some clever coaches led by Duffy
Daugherty, Johnny McKay, and then Bob Devaney, began to
recruit African-American players in large numbers. And many
of the players came from the South.

Historians will scoff at the premise that football helped
to integrate the South and has been an instrumental force in
helping to improve the African-American movement. Football teams have always been a macho symbol of manhood. In
the old days, Kings had their champions to represent them in
games versus adversaries, and even at times fought to the death
to settle disputes. Modern day football has become a symbol

for different areas consisting of people with conflicting ideas. People follow teams with an enthusiasm that borders on mania. An oversimplification would be that if my team beats your team, I am better than you. The quintessential example is Notre Dame with its subway alumni.

When Michigan State, Southern California and Nebraska began to dominate college football in the 1960s, it was because they had a plethora of African-American athletes. Duffy Daugherty of Michigan State, Johnny McKay of Southern California, Bob Devaney of Nebraska, and Bill Yeomans from Houston were all friends of big Bear Bryant. Due to the friendship, their teams decided to play. I believe a turning point in history occurred when John McKay's Southern California team led by Sam "Bam" Cunningham beat the hell out of a "lily white" Alabama squad. Bear Bryant didn't like to lose and he had the foresight to conclude there would be no National Championship coming to Alabama if they didn't recruit some African-American players.

Believe it or not, Bear Bryant used his personal power within the state of Alabama to help get integration implemented. He wanted to keep great African-American athletes in the South. Possibly for selfish motives? But I think deep down inside Bear was a good old boy who always had a vibrant feel for altruistic justice.

I don't know who was directly responsible, but suddenly the top Southern teams began to recruit African-American athletes who now were not only legally admissible but welcomed with open arms. Suddenly in an avalanche, all the southern schools not only allowed African-American student athletes in, but began to heavily recruit them.

In typical southern fervor, the South had turned 180 degrees. From all-white teams they became predominantly African-American. The rage to be number one in football changed everything. Suddenly it was the Eastern teams that had predominantly white teams. The East, who always accepted qualified African-Americans, seemed to be the culprit compared to what the Southern teams were doing. Of course, like Michigan State, Southern California, Nebraska, and Houston, there weren't any stringent academic standards and few people cared if African-Americans graduated. It was blatant hypocrisy. The records corroborated the facts. But the African-American fan didn't know what the truth was.

One Saturday night after a Temple-Penn State game in Philadelphia, and after my TV show, I decided to go back to New York by train. This was a year after Southeast Conference teams were heavily African-American and the Southwest and the Big Eight were close behind. To get to the train station, I jumped into a cab. Because of the exodus of the stadium crowd, the area was filled with people.

Just as my cab was pulling away, a guy knocked on the window. We opened the door and asked where he was going, and he said the train station. I said, "jump in, that's where I'm going". He got in the cab, sat down and introduced himself. He was an African-American whose son went to Penn State but didn't make the team. After telling me about himself and his son, I noticed he looked like he had had a bit to drink.

Without warning he yelled, "I know who you are. You are the brother of that racist coach Joe Paterno". Naturally I was upset. The cab driver was frightened. Before I share my response, it should be pointed out JoPa has faults like all people, but if there is anything he is not, it's racist.

My African-American friend continued, "How come the Southern teams have all those black boys playing and your brother only has a few?" It wasn't the time or place to attempt a philosophical answer, so I only said we were "brought up that there was only one race and that was the human race, so consequently being all equal, no concessions could be made for anyone." In the long run, it would all eventually balance out. He didn't understand. He told the cab driver to stop and he got out.

As I was coming home on the train between the clickity-clack clatter of the train sounds, I couldn't help but be concerned of what my cabmate had said. The South was making guys like Joe look bad. Compared to the Southern coaches,

Joe was Abe Lincoln, but because he was interested in African-American athletes as potential productive students who had to reach for higher goals he was now unfairly being called a racist.

My Dad's African-American friends in the court system and my African-American partner on the New York Police Department, George McQueen, would have vehemently made protest. In the long run, the most distinguished African-American educators and leaders espoused similar views. They wanted African-American students to prove their innate abilities; they would accept minimum admission concessions because of years of deprivation in secondary education, but they wanted to move up and graduate and not be exploited as athletes. Which is exactly what Joe has always believed in and tried to implement. African-American athletes, parents and friends have equal and open access to Joe and Sue's home. In my opinion, the African-Americans who played for Joe represent their race and the university as well, if not better than any other school in the country.

Wouldn't it be wonderful if races had the same respect for each other off the field as they do on the playing field? The give and take on the field is analogous to a laboratory where experiments on human relations are conducted. Respect and compassion are key links to harmonious living conditions. Sure, some athletes don't make it or give sports a bad image (the same exists in any profession) but the good that results from healthy interracial competition far exceeds the bad.

# Chapter Nineteen

# PENN STATE AND THE CONFERENCE

hen it was officially made public that Penn
State would play football in the Big Ten beginning in 1993, a major dichotomy of opin-
ion was expressed by alumni, press, and all Penn State root-
ers. To fit into a Big Ten schedule, some of the old perennial
foes had to be dropped off the schedule. The biggest complaints were related to the termination of competition with
old bitter rivals the University of Pittsburgh, Syracuse, and
West Virginia. A lot of history would be expunged, but Joe,
Jim Tarman, and the president of the school, Dr. Joab Thomas,
thought it to be a good move. Everyone was joining conferences. Penn State wanted to be in a conference where all
sports could participate, especially basketball. Playing as an
independent, Penn State's basketball program was struggling
and could get healthy in the Big Ten. The impact on football
could only be evaluated after a full year of competition. However, the tumult and shouting had begun.

    Some people said Penn State would lose money. Some
said attendance would drop at home. Some said it would hurt
recruiting. Some said the team was not good enough to compete in the Big Ten. Some said Joe betrayed the East, and

there were endless other complaints. At the end of the 1993 season, the answers would be evident.

You couldn't say Penn State had momentum going into the 1993 season after the team collapsed in 1992. Besides having to play a formidable Big Ten schedule, always powerful Southern California was still on the schedule and USC had beaten State in 1990 and 1991. Returning to Southern California as coach was the popular and successful John Robinson.

At the close of spring practice in '92, Kerry Collins looked like he would be the man at quarterback with John Sacca as number two. But Kerry fell victim to bad luck in '92 when he broke his index finger on his passing hand three weeks before preseason practice was to begin. Behind Sacca in '92 was only a true freshman, talented Wally Richardson. Sacca would start at quarterback and everyone hoped Collins would make a speedy recovery.

The team and Sacca got off to a good start in '93, beating Minnesota, 38-20, in the first game. Penn State unleashed a strong passing game led by a new star Bobby Engram and a newly dedicated tight end, Kyle Brady. JoPa used three tailbacks, Mike Archie, Ki-Jana Carter and Mike Pitts. Mount Rushmore looked like it was in good shape. The trio of tailbacks were all good, but one seemed to be a notch above the other two. Ki-Jana Carter from Big Ten territory in Warren, Ohio, had an aura of greatness about him. The fullback was solid with Brian O'Neal, another Ohio player. Penn State's defense had many returnees and was quick but not considered very big. But Minnesota was not a heralded team. They had a wide-open passing game but could not run right at people. And their defense was weak. A more formidable test would come the following week against Southern California.

Coming into Happy Valley to play Penn State, Southern California had three of the premier players in the country at their positions: quarterback Rob Johnson; a flanker, John Morton; and a giant tackle, Tony Boselli. And their defense was much better than Minnesota's. State got off to an early lead, which they held into the fourth quarter. Penn State's defense was doing a fine job controlling Southern California's vaunted passing offense.

Coach Robinson stayed with the pass in the first half, but came out in the second half with a more balanced offense. They began to move the ball, and Penn State was having a problem defensing the run. Southern Cal's defense also tightened up.

Going into the fourth quarter, Southern Cal needed two scores to win. While running the ball, they were taking time off the clock, so time was also in Penn State's favor. So JoPa, also wanting to take time off the clock, wisely did not get reckless. But when he needed completions on third down to keep drives going, Sacca was misfiring, and Southern Cal continued to get the ball back. Penn State hung on to win, 21-20, but one wondered what would have happened if Southern Cal ran the ball early in the game, and you had to question Sacca's inconsistency. Kerry Collins was still rusty, so Joe had concerns about quarterback. If Sacca had made a couple of completions on third downs late in the fourth quarter, Southern California wouldn't have come so close, but a win is a win.

Penn State won handily over the next two opponents, a weak Iowa squad and a rebuilding Rutgers team. The defense had come together and was playing extremely well. But Sacca continued to sputter, and Collins saw some action to get the patina off. Outside of Southern Cal, no team proposed any problems that would be close to what State would face versus the University of Michigan and Ohio State. Following a rout of a pitiful Maryland squad, Penn State once again would be 5-0 going into a big game at home. This time Michigan replaced Miami as the behemoth, and once again JoPa was under pressure to win a big game. Shades of 1992. To compound problems, John Sacca reacted poorly to being replaced by Collins and threatened to quit. So Joe had much to consider getting prepared for Michigan, a preseason pick by many as the best team in the country.

October 16, 1993 was a perfect fall day for football. Undefeated Penn State versus powerful Michigan. Penn State's first year in the Big Ten. A chance to prove Penn State was worthy of being a force in their new conference. A chance to put an end to all the snickers coming from the pompous Big Ten coaches who refused to believe Penn State teams were for real. A win by Penn State certainly would give them a chance to go to the Rose Bowl in their first year as a member of the Big Ten and maybe an undefeated season. Outside of playing for National Championships, it had to be one of Penn State's biggest and most important games ever.

Michigan came to State College loaded for bear. They had a tailback named Tyrone Wheatly, considered by most to be the best in the country. They also had the best quarterback in the Big Ten, Todd Collins, who threw to a swift group of wideouts lead by Derrick Alexander behind a gigantic talented offensive line. Their defense, man for man, was one of the best in the country. What a scenario for college football. Would there be a repeat of the 1992 Miami game, or were JoPa and Penn State back on track? In the past, Joe and Penn State had a reputation for winning big games, especially Bowl Games.

As in the first five games, Penn State took an early lead. They had an excellent offensive game plan and the defense was holding up. Defensively, Penn State, concerned with the great wideout Alexander, played his side soft, using a linebacker to help out in coverage and it seemed to be working. Throughout the first half, Penn State had a decisive edge and things looked good until the first breakdown came. Right before the first half ended, Alexander, who also returned punts, broke a long one for a touchdown. The coverage on one side overran the ball and opened a big seam, and suddenly Michigan had a score. It sure pumped them up going into the locker room at the end of the half.

Coming out for the second half, Michigan seemed confident. Penn State gave them an easy touchdown and they were back in the game. Penn State's fans were uneasy. Michigan was too good to give them anything so easy. Penn State's worst fears came to fruition. On their first possession, Michigan made a nice adjustment and began to run the ball to the short side of their field in the direction of Alexander, who was drawing double coverage. With Wheatly piling up yardage in big chunks, Michigan went in for a score. The silence of the Penn State fans was palpable. They had the dry taste of defeat in their mouths, but the Nittany Lions were not about to quit.

Collins was beginning to jell and the offense was on the move. Penn State drove the ball to Michigan's six-inch line. It was first and goal to go. Armchair quarterbacks always seem to have the answers, but coaches will tell you how tough it is to score, the closer you get to the goal line. Literally, the field shrunk to ten yards and six inches; not much room to operate. If you gamble and go wide and someone on the defense penetrates, it could result in a five-yard loss, and the fans would yell "dumb call". If you passed and for some reason the ball was intercepted, the fans would again roar, "dumb call". After all, you only have six inches to go, and a straight line would be the best direction to go.

In the past, Penn State fans were accustomed to seeing Blair Thomas or Richie Anderson go airborne and vault the line for a few yards. The last time Penn State was stopped this close to a touchdown was in the 1978 Sugar Bowl game against Alabama. Surely the great Ki-Jana Carter could make six inches. Four times Penn State and Carter went straight ahead and four times Michigan stopped them. You're damned if you don't get the touchdown, no matter what play you call. Michigan won the game, 21-13, and the fickle boo-birds began their cackling. Joe couldn't win the big ones anymore. Throw out Alexander's punt return and the Michigan goal line stand, and Penn State would have out-played possibly the number-one team in the country. The trained eye could see Penn State's offense coming together with Collins at the helm. Whether the team would fold or not, like in 1992, could only be speculation. It would be up to the kids.

The worst thing a person or a team can do after a heart-breaking setback is to dwell on the loss. If you don't put the remorse and disappointment behind you, it will break your concentration and carry into the future. JoPa was truly concerned. He had to be apprehensive of how his team would react.

The next game would be powerful Ohio State on their home field. Coach Cooper of Ohio State was constantly being assailed by Ohio State fans. They were used to Woody Hayes and not only Big Ten Championships, but National Championships. Coach Cooper was quoted as saying this 1993 squad was the most talented he had since being appointed head coach. Offensively, Ohio State was gigantic. Their tackles, Springer and Winnrow, made pro scouts drool. Quarterback Hoying and flanker Galloway were as good as anyone in the country.

On the defensive side of the ball, Ohio State also had great players. One of their tackles, Big Daddy Wilkerson, was considered the best in the country and the linebackers and secondary were unparalleled. If Penn State was to have a good chance to win, they must take advantage in the one area they were superior, team speed.

Lined up man for man, Ohio State would have a 20- to 25-pound weight advantage. Boy, did the Nittany Lions need a dry day. What they got was Mother Nature at her worst.

Game day, a late afternoon would be JoPa's worst nightmare. With field lights on because of the late start, the mixture of snow, hail, and rain on a freezing afternoon was tearing the field to pieces. It would be the worst of weather conditions for Penn State. Their team speed would be diminished by the muddy field. As giant chunks of turf were kicked around, all the sophisticated techniques and strategy were neutralized. The game evolved into the bigger body concept. A smaller, courageous Penn State squad went down to defeat, 24-6. As in 1992, after winning the first five games, there were two consecutive losses. A repeat of the 1992 collapse? The bombast from the Big Ten coaches was, "I told you so," alluding to Penn State being overrated. But much was to be learned;

as compared to '92, this Penn State squad was younger and played with more intensity. A few mistakes beat them versus Michigan, and Mother Nature welcomed them to her capricious whimsical Midwestern weather elements. Moreover, JoPa learned from the two best teams in the Big Ten. They liked their players huge and would love to beat the opponents physically if they could. To play man-to-man, smashmouth football was what they liked and wanted. It was time to change and go to brains over brawn.

This was not going to be a repeat of 1992. They were led by co-captains Benfatti, Malinoski, and O'Neal, newly entrenched quarterback Collins and the reincarnated tight end named Brady. Along with the mercurial trio of Carter, Engram and Scott, Penn State would win all the remaining games, including  a great come-from-behind win over Michigan State, 38-37, and a smashing defeat of Tennessee in the Citrus Bowl, 31-13. The Nittany Lions won the last five games in a row, averaging 35.9 points per game.

Joe Paterno once again displayed his chameleon personality. Old, conservative, Jurassic Joe had opened up his mind and changed his offensive philosophical strategy. Don Coryell (air-Coryell) of the fabled San Diego teams would have done a "double take" and been impressed. Paterno had gone airborne. If you can't run over them, fly over them. And if you make a game plan with that in mind, you might end up doing both.

After the Tennessee Bowl victory, everyone would start counting the days waiting for 1994. After the rust wore off Kerry Collins, he played quarterback with impelling dedication and Joe Montana-style  execution. With the speed guys, Carter, Engram, Scott, and a great offensive line led by tight end Kyle Brady, the incarnate of "Finn McCool" (of Irish folklore), the Lions had manhandled Tennessee, a team who at the end of the year was considered by many as the best. No wonder everyone was salivating thinking about 1994. After all, in its first year in the Big 10, Penn State came in second, losing only to Michigan and Ohio State, and won its last five games in a row. Most important, they would have almost everyone back in 1994. And Byzantine Joe would know what to expect from his new Big 10 opponents. He was willing to switch from a Chevy to a Ferrari to get where he wanted to go. Pasadena!

# Chapter Twenty

# PASADENA AND ROSES

Spring practice is used to look at new players and make position shifts that will be beneficial to the team. Fundamentals are emphasized, and at the end of practice, the coach likes to have a good idea who will be his top 22 players on offense and defense.

And of course, who will handle the vitally important kicking game? In the last five games of the '93 season, the offense averaged over 35 points per game. But JoPa and the staff still looked for improvement. A couple of moves in the offensive line established a group that would turn out to be one of the best in the country.

Greely, Johnson, Rivera, Hartings and Conlin could be the best ever. Kyle Brady had come into his own and was considered by most experts as the best blocking tight end in the country. Brady and Fred Scott were given additional responsibilities in the passing game. All the running backs would return, and full backs Witman and Milne would more than compensate for the departing Brian O'Neil. Most important, the quarterback position was stable and in the hands of Kerry Collins. For the offense to continue where it left off in '93, Collins would have to perform as he did in the latter part of '93.

On paper, the defense looked stronger than in '93. The down people, Stewart, Thomas, Claire, Perry, Mazyck and Odom would supply more beef than the prior year. The linebackers were experienced, led by Gelzheiser, one of the best in the country. And the secondary was developing cohesiveness. Newcomer Herring looked good and there was a lot of experience at cornerback with Forbes, Pittman, Miller, Tate and Collins. It seemed the only thing that could derail this squad in 1994 would be injuries.

In 1994, Penn State would open up at Minnesota against a squad that was vastly improved and then return home to play three consecutive games. For the first home game, Southern Cal would be the opponent, the preseason pick to win the powerful Pac 10. Next would be Big 10 rival, Iowa, who is always tough; followed by old Eastern foe Rutgers.

On September 3, 1994, Penn State unleashed what was to become one of the greatest offensive machines ever to play the game of football. Penn State beat Minnesota, 56-3. It was a total team victory. The nonbelievers demurred and said, "Yes, but Minnesota wasn't any good". Wait till next week, things would be different against tough Southern Cal. The score of that contest: Penn State 38, Southern Cal 14, but it really wasn't that close. Penn State was up by five scores in the first half. The offense was unstoppable, and the defense adequate. I think even Joe and his staff were shocked at how quickly the offense could score. I remember saying to my radio partner, Fran Fisher, that I had "never seen a team score so fast". The execution of offense was borderline "perfect" and Kerry Collins did look like Joe Montana.

As always with a big lead early in the game, Joe substitutes a great deal to give young players experience, and it has always paid dividends as the season progressed. Coach Robinson was in a state of shock; he thought he had an outstanding defense. Robinson stated on that day that Penn State had the most awesome offense he had ever seen. And it was only the beginning. Iowa was the next team to come to Happy Valley.

In an unbelievable demonstration of offensive football, Penn State clobbered a perennial strong Iowa team, 61-21. Like John Robinson the week before, the highly respected Hayden Frye from Iowa said he had "never seen such a potent offense".

Once again the defense was adequate, but who had to play defense when you had such a great offense? However, it was the beginning of a series of injuries to the defense that might cause some problems if the offense faltered. Stewart, Claire, and Thomas were injured, all down line men, the one position where Penn State lacked depth. Some of the secondary were getting bumps and bruises too.To achieve cohesion, whether it be offense or defense, the same players need to constantly play together.

Although the defense began to suffer injuries, the offense stayed healthy and continued to get better each week. They were scoring at such a frenetic clip, that on more than one occasion, before some of the defensive players coming off the field on a change of possession could get to the water fountain for a drink, the offense had scored again.

As the defensive players returned to the fray, running by their offensive teammates, some humorous curse words were exchanged, translated to mean, "Hey! Give us a break." Especially early in the season in the hot and humid weather.

Going into the fourth game against Rutgers, Penn State had captured the imaginations of the fans and the sports media. They were scoring more points at a faster rate than anyone in history. Could they keep it up?

Coach Graber of Rutgers, like Coach Wacker of Minnesota, told the press his team was vastly improved and ready to challenge for the Big East title. Plus, Rutgers always tried a little harder against Penn State.The final score was Penn State 55, Rutgers 27 in a perfunctory win with Joe emptying the bench.

The players, remembering '93, had to be looking ahead to Michigan in the "Big House" at Ann Arbor. "Be careful," Joe said, an improving Temple team had to be laying in ambush before the trip to Michigan.

Temple was coached by one of Joe's former assistants and one of the first African-Americans to coach a major team, Ron Dickerson. He was a class person and he was instilling that class to the Temple program. And I am sure Joe remembered the 1988 season when former assistant Dick Anderson coaching Rutgers orchestrated an upset that led to Joe's first and only losing season. On a miserable, foggy, rainy night, Penn State prevailed, 48-21, against a well-coached, feisty Temple squad. The outcome was never in doubt, but it was the Nittany Lions' poorest performance of the year and was compounded by an injury to Ki-Jana Carter's right thumb. Thanks to an open date, the Michigan game would be two weeks later.

Having been an assistant coach at Michigan State, I knew how tough it would be to beat Michigan in Ann Arbor. If there are two teams in the country that take pride in defending their football prestige at home, they're Notre Dame with "Touchdown Jesus" and Michigan in their "Big House". Both teams have intensely loyal fans who make a lot of noise. The drums were beating along the Great Lakes. If Michigan could handle Penn State in Pennsylvania, beating them in front of 100,000 plus fans should be no problem.

Coach Moeller said Penn State's offensive machine would come to an abrupt halt in the "Big House". Michigan's Coach Moeller and his predecessor Bo Schembechler had little respect for the Nittany Lions. It would be fun when the Wolverines once again stuck it to the Lions. Part of Michigan's confidence was related to Penn State's rash of defensive injuries that made them vulnerable.

On October 15, 1994, Joe Paterno, his staff, and squad once and for all underlined in capital letters, put in italics, and punctuated the quality of Penn State football.

It was a perfect day for the game and the 106,832 fans present agreed. Joe and his staff did a great job preparing the team, not only to play the game but to handle the crowd. The first half was almost a replica of '93—Penn State, ignoring the boos of the hostile crowd, went about their business and took command of the game, gaining an early lead going into the second half. But the Michigan squad and their fans weren't worried. They remembered the Nittany Lions' first-half lead in 1993, and Tyrone Wheatly was back in form. Wheatly had missed the early games with a shoulder problem but he was ably replaced by Tim Biakabatuka, so now Michigan had two great tailbacks.

Although beat up, Penn State's defense was playing well, but so did they in 1993. It was deja-vu early in the second half when Penn State's defense gambled, got caught in a blitz, and Wheatly made a long run for a touchdown. Michigan was one touchdown from the lead. Mixing the passing of their quarterback Todd Collins and the running of the two tailbacks, Michigan was wearing down the injured Penn State defense as they did in 1993.

It looked like a repeat of '93. As the game seesawed, Penn State's offense continued to put pressure on Michigan's offense to do as well. Which they did; late in the fourth quarter, Penn State's offense was faced with the quintessential "gut check"—the game was tied 24-24 with seven minutes to go. If Kerry Collins and his teammates wanted the national recognition they hungered for, they would have to put together a long drive, take time off the clock and get to football's metaphorical "house", known as the end zone in Michigan's "Big House".

In a drive that coaches dream of, Penn State, led by Kerry Collins, chopped away at a superior Michigan defense, expunging the crowd noise, and put the ball in the "Big House". It was a disciplined drive, executed by each and every man on the offense. It was not the quick strike for the big touchdown; it was a mixed bag of pass, run, pass, deception, power and victory. One had to think back to 1992—this was a different team, this was true Penn State football! This was a Joe Paterno team! A team like 1968-'69, only the emphasis was on offense.

Next up was Ohio State. If ever a game galvanized a team to go on to greatness, it would be similar to Penn State versus Michigan in 1994—Bring on Ohio State!!!

On that rainy, snowy, foggy evening at Columbus in 1993, Penn State not only lost by points, they were beaten up physically. Coming off the field at the end of the game, the players were subject to ridicule and taunts by the Ohio State team. They weren't "Lions", they were "pussy cats" who had no business trying to play with the "big boys".

All that animosity that had been seething for a year erupted on October 29 at Beaver Stadium. The "pussy cats", with elephantine memories, humiliated basically the same Ohio State team that maligned them in '93. The score was 63-14 and could have been higher if Joe wanted to be vindictive. A volcano of Nittany Lion pride had erupted and once emotions flowed, only the final whistle would terminate the massacre.

Coach Cooper from Ohio State was speechless. The game was on national TV for all the world to see. The fickle, vacillating media were effusive in their praise and were looking for new adjectives to describe Penn State's spectacular offensive performance. The ghost of '93 was gone forever. The fact that some narrow-minded writers (four from Ohio) refused to vote Penn State as the number-one team really didn't matter. The most important people, the team, knew what they had accomplished. They were the toast of the sports world. Four more wins and the smell of roses would permeate the air in Happy Valley.

It's ironic and sickening to think one of the weakest teams on the schedule, Indiana, might have cost the Lions a National Championship. The game was played in front of only 47,754 fans at Indiana, and in some respects, it was an easy game for Penn State. Sure, there may have been a bit of a let down after the consecutive dramatic victories over Michigan and Ohio State, but the Nittany Lions were totally in control and victory was never in doubt. Sometimes someone must pay a price to illuminate certain growing ills in any area, especially in sports. One of the venerable, compelling aphorisms in sports is not to humiliate a beaten opponent. Good sportsmanship means if you can help it, you don't deliberately embarrass the other team.

Penn State took an early, dominating lead versus Indiana and held it with only eight minutes remaining in the game. Joe was content to play with substitutes for most of the second half. The game was dull until the end. Indiana scored 21 points in the final seven minutes, and 14 in the last two minutes, with their last touchdown scored on the last play of the game. When Indiana got their second score, State had 35 points. Joe easily could have put the first string back into the game, but he didn't care much about the margin of victory. So the subs remained in the game as Indiana was allowed to make the score look respectable.

For espousing and practicing true sportsmanship, Penn State was punished by hypocritical pollsters who didn't see the game and lost their number-one ranking in both the coaches' and the A.P. Writers polls. Anyone who saw the game knew Penn State could have scored 50 points or more. But as JoPa says, we can't worry about other people's business, we have to take care of our own.

The following week would be Illinois in Champaign, and Penn State's defense continued to be plagued by injuries. Getting ready for Illinois, Penn State had seven defensive starters miss one to five games. It's tough to develop cohesion when each week different players are used. Also, the Illinois defense was second ranked in the nation and maybe deserved to be first. The contest would seem to focus on the Nittany Lions' number-one rated offense against the Illinois vaunted defense, led by Simeon Rice and the best linebackers corps in the country.

If you believe in astrology, horoscopes, destiny, or bad vibes, you will enjoy knowing what actually happened on the weekend of November 12. It is most unusual for a visiting team to stay on or near the campus of the home team. Because of a lack of available facilities and an expected sell-out crowd of over 70,000, Penn State did just that. The coach and staff work hard getting the team mentally as well as physically prepared for the game. Against a worthy opponent, physical preparation alone won't suffice. In fact, more big games are decided by cerebral preparation and execution. So it is vital that a team not be subject to outside distractions.

I arrived at the hotel Friday afternoon before the team. The place was pulsating with a mix of Illinois and Penn State fans. Quarters were close and located on the perimeter of the campus. Not knowing the lack of facility problems, I said to myself, "Joe must be nuts". I had seen Illinois on TV and this was going to be a tough game.

Their defense flew to the ball and blitzed like hell with great alacrity. And their offense had some big-play guys, especially quarterback Johnny Johnson and running back Ty Douthard. Coach Lou Tepper was an extremely effective motivator with a cerebral approach to the game of football. You just knew Illinois was ready to spring an upset. Penn State would have to concentrate to get the job done. As far as I was concerned, they had already gotten off to a bad start by staying in a disruptive locale. I kept thinking how fishermen "chum" to catch sharks. That hotel smelled of "chum". Boy, were my vibes right.

The team checked in late Friday as they always do on away games. Frank Rocca, an associate Athletic Director who is one of the unsung heroes behind the scenes was ever present, directing the assignment of rooms and facilitating making everyone comfortable. No one realized what would happen once the players were settled in. I saw Joe and could tell he was perplexed; he didn't like the scenario. Although the accommodations couldn't be helped, Joe also smelled the "chum".

Being an old bachelor who lived by the water between two boat marinas, I have become an early riser. As usual I was up, had taken my daily walk, and read the papers before the kitchen was open for breakfast. I sat in the lobby for a while and at precisely 8:00 a.m. went to the only dining hall for breakfast. It was on the top floor in the hotel. The view was nice, but more suited for dinner. While perusing the breakfast menu, the newly appointed Athletic Director, Tim Curley, came in with Budd Thallman, Associate Director in charge of Media

Affairs. They joined me; we ordered breakfast and talked a bit about the game. The team's routine for the day would be an optional early brunch or to sleep in with an arranged pre-game meal. Everything seemed to be in order until I asked for the check. It was minimal, so I gave the waitress a $20 bill and told my companions we would even matters out later. We continued to make small conversation; I called the manager over and asked why the delay. It was then the fiasco began and the "chum" got thicker.

The manager said the waitress had to walk 20 floors below to get change because the elevators were out from a power shortage. The floor below us was to be set up for brunch and eventually the pregame meal. I told Curly someone should call Joe, because this could be a problem. You don't want players walking up 20 floors and down again on the day of the game. Well, my premonition was right. There had been a major power outage in the entire area, and not only were the elevators out, all electrical conduits would be unusable for an undetermined amount of time. No elevators, no breakfast, no pregame meal, no pregame meetings; a total disruption of the important game-day routine.

The residents of the hotel were in a state of semi-panic, some of the guests were parents and friends of the Penn State players. All that was needed to further disrupt the concentration of a team vying for a National Championship would be an earthquake. Meanwhile, it would be a serene, normal day for the Fighting Illini. The "chum" was working, and the Penn State prey was closer to being hooked.

Entering the stadium would be a Penn State team who ate pizza for its pregame meal and had worried about parents. Coach Tepper couldn't have planned a better way to disrupt the team. You could almost feel in the pregame warm up a sense of major distraction among the Penn State team. While the Nittany Lions seemed lugubrious in the pregame drills, the Illini came on the field in a frenzy, led by Coach Tepper running with a sprinter's speed. Joe gave him a side glance and smirked, but he knew he and his team were victims of the unforeseen, uncontrollable, whims of fortune. All his knowledge and experience would be tested this day.

Coming into the game, Illinois was not considered a good running team, even though their Tailback Ty Douthard was exceptional. The offensive coordinator, Greg Landry, was an experienced pro quarterback and liked the passing game. But not this day. Maybe it was the weak Penn State defense.

Penn State won the toss and elected to receive. The return was not a good one, only getting back to the 18-yard line. Illinois came down the field like a pack of wild dogs on route to a kill. Whether the systematic series of disruptions State was exposed to would affect them would soon be known.

On their second play from scrimmage, the normally reliable Kijani Carter fumbled, and Illinois recovered on Penn State's 20. The Illinois fans went wild. The battered Penn State defense would be put to the test early in the game. The scenario for the classic upset that began on Friday afternoon continued to evolve.

After getting the ball, Illinois stunned the Nittany Lions by going to an unexpected power running game. Douthard and the offensive line made it look easy as Illinois scored on it first possession and led, 7-0.

It's not unusual for a team to get behind after an early turnover, but on this occasion Penn State fans had to be concerned. It seemed nothing could go right for the Lions. And things would get worse. The great Illini defense again stopped the best offense in the country that seemed to be confused and playing in a catatonic state.

Running the ball, Illinois took a commanding 21-0 lead going into the second quarter. I thought about my initial feelings coming into the hotel. If it was a set-up initiated by a mix of unfortunate circumstances, it didn't make any difference. The great Penn State team seemed to be just going through the motions.

Sometimes when people are subjected to an unexpected series of events, they go into a semi-trance. Only a severe shock can bring them back to reality. Being behind 21-0, the players didn't need to be motivated by coaches, they came out of their somnolence by themselves. Thoroughbreds, whether animals or man, when sensing defeat, reach into a reservoir of energy and intrinsic karma and make a run to win.

Behind 21-0 at the end of the first quarter, the situation looked hopeless. Then the sleeping lions awoke. Penn State scored twice in the second quarter, but Illinois also scored. At halftime, Illinois led, 28-14. Was it too late? Remember, the Illinois defense was ranked number two in the country. State surely had a formidable task ahead of them.

The second half began, and Illinois quickly kicked a field goal to lead, 31-14. Penn State's offense responded and scored a touchdown, making the score 31-21 at the end of the third quarter. JoPa and his team still needed two touchdowns to win and they had only 15 minutes to do so. Illinois would have to be immediately stopped and the Lions couldn't make any errors. To make matters worse, the wind had picked up on this late fall afternoon and Penn State had it blowing right into their faces. But these thoroughbred athletes drove the ball down the field and the big FB Milne crashed over from the five. Now the score was Illinois 31, Penn State 28, but the drive took time off the clock.

To make the unbelievable comeback and win with the wind and clock against them seemed impossible. The drive against Michigan had begun with seven minutes to go and no wind. Penn State would get one more chance to keep the "Impossible Dream" alive. The Lions' defense rose to the occasion stimulated by the play of the offense, and stopped Illinois with just over four minutes left in the game. Penn State fans were hoping for a bad punt or a great return by Mike Archie who was back to receive the punt.

The fans' hopes went up in smoke. With the wind at his back, the Illinois punter boomed one that got caught in the high swirling atmosphere. Archie misjudged the ball, it sailed over his head and was blown dead on Penn State's 3-yard line. Since Friday, misfortune had beleaguered JoPa and his squad, and this last bad break seemed to be the death knell.

Ninety-seven yards to go in four minutes, into a tough swirling wind, against a great defense that were on a feeding frenzy, smelling victory, seemed insurmountable even for this great Penn State offense. Had they just waited too long to come alive? Or did this big fish who seemed to be hooked have a few jumps left and could spit out the hook?

Coming out of the huddle were eleven determined young men. With the wind as the 12th man, play selection would be paramount. It would be tough to get a big play, and the clock had to be always involved in the call.

Down the field they came. First Carter, for short yardage and then again for a first down. One could hear the pads popping and the noise of the collisions in the stands. This was brutal, smashmouth football. No one was blinking on either side. Still the Lions, chunk by chunk, moved down the field. A third-down completion to Engram, after an Illinois blitz that almost knocked Collins down kept the drive going.

Knowing the difficulty of throwing into the wind, Illinois Coach Tepper unleashed his great corps of linebackers, who were blitzing on every play from every angle. Just one Penn State mistake was all Illinois needed for the upset. And the tick-tick of the clock could almost be heard like church bells at a funeral. The Lions, approaching mid-field, again needed a first down or it was over. Again the blitz, again Collins under duress hit his big tight end Brady who made a clutch catch.

The clock showed two minutes left. Joe Paterno handles the sidelines and the two-minute drill better than any coach in the country, so they had sufficient time-outs left to stretch that two minutes to three. But they still needed a big chunk. Now the Lions were threatening, and the Illinois defense had to be careful. Next came a beautifully called draw play and another sizeable gain. If there was no panic and the clock was used fortuitously, State could go back to the run, which they did.

With 44 seconds to go, the ball rested on the Illinois two-yard line. And with time running out, Brian Milne scored the winning touchdown. To say it was unbelievable is close to the truth. With players like Milne who didn't quit when he was diagnosed with Hodgkins disease, leading the way, the Lions escaped the trap, spit out the "hook" and would now only have to beat Northwestern and Michigan State to have an undefeated season and go to Pasadena. Lombardi once said when "things get tough, the tough get going." Kerry Collins and company must have heard Lombardi in one ear and JoPa in the other as he drove his team to victory.

Penn State would end this phenomenal season with wins over Northwestern and Michigan State. To the amazement of the sports pundits and the Big 10 coaches, JoPa and the "pussy cats" won the Big 10 conference in their second year and won with an undefeated season. To put the so-called "frosting on the cake," they would have to beat a good Oregon team in the Rose Bowl.

# Chapter Twenty-one

# A ROSE BY ANY NAME

The two most difficult games to prepare for in a season are the first and last, if the last is a Bowl game. No matter how many years you coach, and regardless of how the team practices, you can't be sure of their initial performance. A Bowl game is similar, but different. Similar, because of the long lay off between the last game and the Bowl game; sometimes as much as five weeks. Proper conditioning and timing again become important factors. Different, because a coach has seen his team play a full schedule and knows a great deal about their strengths and weaknesses, and what can be expected if he gets them ready to play at their best. So JoPa and staff had to plan how to keep this potent offense razor sharp and to get more cohesion from a defense that would benefit injury wise from rest.

Finishing unbeaten in their second year in the Big 10 was quite an accomplishment for the Lions. In doing so, they set many records for a Penn State team and a Big 10 team.

With five offensive players picked as All-Americans, Collins, Carter, Bradley, Engram and Hartings, they broke ten school records. Some were total offense: 5,722 yards, points: 526, and points per game: 47.8. Big 10 records also were set in points per game: 48.1. Kerry Collins surpassed Michigan's

Jim Harbaugh for pass efficiency with a 172.86 grade; Harbaugh had 163.7. Place kicker Brett Conway's 62 PATS became a new record. Other records also were set for total offense: 5,722 yards, 520.2 yards per game, 7.64 yards per play, 526 total points, 47.8 points per game, and of course, 71 touchdowns. Going into the Rose Bowl, Joe had a chance to surpass Bear Bryant for the most Bowl victories and also to become the first coach in history to win all the major Bowls.

The Oregon game loomed as a difficult contest; the Ducks had easily beaten a strong Washington team who beat up on Miami in Florida. Not easy to do. Miami would play Nebraska who was ranked number one in the Orange Bowl, so a possible National Championship could also be riding on the outcome of the Rose Bowl.

Coach Brooks of Oregon had a great reputation as a solid coach. His forte was a speedy defense that featured a great deal of blitzing; much like Illinois. And the strongest part of the defense was the secondary, who could match up well with State's receivers Engram and Scott. Odds makers had Penn State an early heavy favorite, and JoPa was concerned but knew this squad would be mature enough not to take Oregon lightly. His real worry was he knew an offense can easily lose that precise timing needed for big plays, especially in the passing game. And an offensive line can also lose cohesiveness needed to pick up all the stunts and blitzes that he knew Oregon would use.

Byzantine Joe really wanted the team ready for this Bowl. Aside from the personal records, a victory would give him an undefeated season, and possibly a National Championship was at stake.

The Nittany Lions arrived in California earlier than they had for any previous Bowls. After all, this was California, known for Hollywood, earthquakes, forest fires, floods and mud slides, so it would be prudent to be ready for all contingencies. (Illinois proved that).

The Penn State team stayed at three different hotels. The first after the arrival was near the beach and the practice was easy and the players had some fun. After all it had been a brilliant but tough year, and they earned some recreation.

The second week the team was moved to a hotel away from the water and nearer to the practice field. Practices became more intense as the countdown to the game began. During the second week, I visited a few practices and the offense looked a bit rusty, especially Kerry Collins. Knowing Oregon would take many reckless chances on defense, everyone was apprehensive. Fortunately as practice wound down, Kerry began to regain his form. The night before the game, JoPa took his squad to a third hotel in the city near the stadium. It was a quiet place where the players could concentrate on the job ahead.

Because January 1 fell on a Sunday, the game was played on January 2. The night before, Nebraska had beaten Miami in the Orange Bowl, and the media claimed Nebraska National Champions. Naturally, the Penn State team saw the game and had to be disappointed, and they still had to face an underestimated Oregon who had everything to gain and nothing to lose.

The weather for the game was absolutely perfect; a beautiful sunny day accompanied by a cool breeze. Oregon took the opening kickoff and with a precision short passing game moved smartly down the field but missed a field goal. Penn State took over, and on the second play Carter broke loose for an 83-yard touchdown. It looked too easy. But Oregon responded with a touchdown. Their All-Pac-10 quarterback O'Neil was hot. The Lions outscored Oregon, 7-0, in the second quarter, and led 14-7 at the half. No doubt the offense was sputtering, but the defense was playing well. The Ducks had come to play.

JoPa and his staff made some half-time adjustments and the offense got their seasonal rhythm back, and the Nittany Lions won going away, 38-20. A cherry was put on the icing, but they would finish number two in the polls. Not fair, but true. And now Joe was getting a new nickname, "The Lion King".

# Chapter Twenty-two

# POLLSTERS AND SOPHISTRY

Who was number one in 1994—Nebraska or Penn State? The AP writers poll and the coaches poll picked Nebraska number one, Penn State number two. The *New York Times* computer poll and the Saberin *USA Today* poll, picked Penn State number one, Nebraska number two. Which poll was correct?

Before dissecting the absurd sophistry used in determining the final selection, let us emphatically state that when you have two undefeated major powers ranked one and two, the issue should be focused on why they aren't allowed to determine who is best on the field, and not have one team suffer unjustly as a victim of politics based on shallow, fallacious reasoning. The present method used by the two major polls, the AP and coaches poll, are void of true dialectic reasoning.

Nebraska vs. Penn State? Take your choice. One of the great college offenses of all time vs. a solid offensive team with an outstanding defense. Before revealing the unjust process that is used in polls, and the hypocritical rationale preventing a playoff, certain essential facts must be pointed out. Penn State, in the years 1967-68, were undefeated and voted number two once, and number three once. Some of the players on those teams, who were not declared national champions, became All-Pro Hall of Famers. It is doubtful any team would have beaten those teams head to head. I am sure this would  be the case for other great college teams that were undefeated and not selected as number one.

Let us look now at why the methodology of present major polls is ludicrous and based on fallacious reasoning. The poll committees are staffed with voters who lack expertise and empirical information, and also lack sufficient analysis and study.

The AP writers poll—what a sham! Sportswriters are like most other professionals, some are good and some are bad. Most members have never played or coached football. They vicariously identify with the sport, and most have never really been involved with the sport in depth. Also, as writers, they are either covering a game personally, or watching or listening to several broadcasts each week. They absolutely do not have the time to carefully evaluate, i.e., "break down films" of all the top teams. They rely on the number of victories, winning margins, alleged severity of schedules, and bombast from TV sport shows, staffed by people who have dubious credentials as experts, for example, fired coaches, clownish and capricious media stooges and some ex-players. All are engaged in hyperbole and media politics based on possible bowl games, with the bottom line being network ratings.

To be more specific, the AP writers, being human, are filled with human imperfections. As in all politics, their vote is based on personal sensitivities, geographic and conference favoritisms, and even reveal ethnic and religious prejudices. After Penn State beat Ohio State 63-14, a real rout, four voters from Ohio State, AP writers and voters—who picked Penn State to finish low in the Big Ten and to be beaten decisively by Ohio State—voted Nebraska number one after Penn State's great victory. The same would apply for several Big East writers who resented Penn State not going into the Big East and deciding on going into the Big Ten. They also voted Penn State number two. Politics should stay in Washington. Joe Paterno is not naive, and he understands the situation. Both he and Tom Osborne agree there should have been a playoff. Why don't the AP writers concentrate on the unjust, hypocritical President's Commission decision that prevents a game playoff? A good investigative sports reporter could undercover the truth.

Now let's look at the coaches poll. The coaches poll is made up of a mix of coaches from different conferences, different areas, and some independents. An article that I read in the *Los Angeles Times* vindicating the AP voting of Penn State as number two stated, "The coaches poll of experts agree with the AP, so the AP writers have to be right".

It was naive of the Los Angeles writer to assume that the coaches' vote is strictly objective. Let's agree that all of the coaches are endowed with expertise, certainly more than the writers. But they, too, lack empirical information because they are far too busy to gather it. Where are the coaches on game day? They are coaching their own teams. Coaches see fewer football games than any fan, let alone the top teams. Good coaches are preparing for the next week's games. They may catch a night game on TV after their afternoon game, but I guarantee that if they play at night, they are not watching TV in the afternoon. And even if they catch a game once in a while, they certainly are not going to see the top teams more than once or twice a year. This is far short of what would be required for them to make an expert decision.

Let's face it. Coaches generally utilize the methods and the same information as the writers do. Very little subjective study is involved. To compound the problem, members of the coaches poll are not "Knights of the Round Table". They are trying to survive in a pressure profession with a dog-eat-dog mentality, especially when it comes to recruiting. Some coaches would not have voted Penn State number one even if they won all of their games by 100 points. Being chosen number one is a great sales pitch in recruiting. To believe that all of the Big East, Big Ten, and independent coaches who have to not only play Penn State, or certainly recruit vs. them, are going to vote them number one for idealistic reasons is naive. Nebraska is not the same formidable competitor because of its location.

Coaches are aware of the imperfections in the system and accept the results, but most would like their players to have the right to decide the championship on the field. The computers who pick polls use the same information, and are not subject to human error. They picked Penn State number one. If you went to Las Vegas and asked for a line on an imaginary Nebraska-Penn State game after the bowls, Penn State would have been favored by seven points and no worse than even money. The powers who represent the bowls in the NCAA admit that the system is imperfect but that it is the only one we have. Is that really true? Why not have a playoff?

The intent here is not to proclaim who was the National Champion. The two teams, Nebraska and Penn State were both great teams, and their coaches are outstanding as well. The intent is to expose the realities of why there isn't a playoff, and the spurious conclusions of polls whose mechanical and emotional conclusions are imperfect at best.

To tell an athlete who has never lost that he is inferior to an unknown adversary could be a death knell to the true substance of what sportsmanship alleges to be. Whatever happened to the fields of friendly strife? By not having a playoff in Division I football, we are slowly but surely destroying the last vestige of altruistic competition left. Because of the great potential profits, the TV moguls, with the assistance of wealthy chambers of commerce who affect gubernatorial elections, who in turn control college subsidies and college presidents may be destroying the last remnants of the American Way: head-to-head competition.

Just imagine if they tried to establish the number one team in professional football without a playoff. A champion means number one. To appoint a champion in sports by use of polls violates the true meaning extended by the concept of intrinsic sportsmanship and the decision must be considered a flagrant oxymoron in the sports world.

To deny a playoff to Division I football when every other sport at every other level has one, should not be tolerated. Fans, get to your writing utensils and voice your views!

While I was pursuing my life as "Larry", Joe was accumulating outstanding records. No matter what your opinion of Joe Paterno or Penn State is, empirical facts cannot be denied. The approaching 1997 season will be JoPa's 32nd year as head coach, and look what he has accomplished. In his tenure, he's had five undefeated untied teams. An astonishing 16 of his teams have finished with 10 or more victories in a season. His teams have won a total of 289 games, the most of any active coach. He has won the most Bowl games (18), and is the only coach to win all the major Bowls. Byzantine Joe won two national championships and had three other undefeated teams that may have been the best in the land. Joe is the only coach to be voted coach of the year four times by his coaching peers. *Sports Illustrated* voted him "Sportsman of the Year" in 1986, the first college football coach to be so honored. The boy from Brooklyn is the only active coach to be honored by the College Football Foundation with its "Distinguished American" Award.

In addition to producing 65 first-team All-Americans and more than 100 professional players, he prides himself on the 20 first-team Academic All-Americans, 12 Hall of Fame scholar-athletes, and 17 postgraduate scholarship winners.

Joe puts his money where his mouth is. He chaired the "Campaign for the Libraries", which generated almost 14 million dollars and he found time to be Vice Chairman of a $350 million drive for Penn State. Another pet project he's involved in is the Bryce Jordan Center. Joe and his wife Sue have donated $250,000 to the Paterno Libraries endowment and had the new wing named after them. All of his records, like DiMaggio's 56-game consecutive hitting streak may never be surpassed.

# Chapter Twenty-three

# THE LION KING

W hen Shakespeare said, "All the world is a stage and the people players", he must have had Joe Paterno in mind. But I think the incomparable Shakespeare was referring to one individual representing a generic type with one personality that explains his character.

Not very often do Shakespearean characters display multiple-sided personalities. Their roles maintain a singularity throughout his plays. The old and famous actor Lon Chaney was known as the "Man of a Thousand Faces", alluding to his versatility as a performer. Can healthy humans display several personalities that surface at different times in different situations?

In his personal odyssey from a skinny adolescent, Joe has made his way from an anonymous middle-class boy from Brooklyn to a man of national stature. He has achieved fame and fortune with "noblesse oblige" and has left an indelible record and message for people not only in his profession but throughout all society. To complete his journey, Joe utilized all of his profound genetic instincts to stay on course.

Many legendary people go through life with one benign title, e.g., "Pop" Warner, "Bear" Bryant, Joe "Yankee Clipper" DiMaggio, Casey "Professor" Stengel, Gen. George "Blood and Guts" Patton, and on and on. During his career, from a young assistant to one of the all-time greats, Joe Paterno has carried numerous sobriquets: Joe "The Wop"; "Don Quixote"; Joe "The Manipulator"; Joe "The Moralist"; "Jurassic Joe"; plain "JoPa" and currently "The Lion King". Each moniker could be correlated to different stages of advancement in his career.

Once again it would seem destiny would get involved in Joe's career. When he won his first National Championship in 1982, his fans discarded the title of "Don Quixote" the dreamer for "JoPa" the forceful conqueror of Miami in 1986. In 1994, while the Lions were battling for honor and recognition in the Big Ten and on a national level, a very popular animated film was released and became a big hit, called "The Lion King". Coincidentally or not, the team saw the film and were startled and impressed that much of the dialogue from this movie had been heard before on the practice field, team meetings and in talks. The spokesman was their coach, Joe. "Don't forget who you are", "Don't forget where you come from" and "Love each other" were familiar terms. So it was the team of '94 who in a private ceremony of spirit and soul, knighted Joe Paterno "The Lion King"—a title he appreciates above all others, except GrandPa.

Every time a problem occurred from the time he decided to join Rip, to his present elevated status, Joe's Byzantine atavistic, genetic instincts surfaced and helped him to overcome adversity. He truly is a man of many faces, a complex character whose computer mind could alert him to all hidden dangers and confrontations that had to be overcome.

What will he need for the future? Joe Paterno, currently football's "Lion King," is 70 years old. Is he looking for a grandiose exit to seek the "Golden Years?"

The "Golden Years", according to philosophers and writers, are the time for a person to terminate employment and settle down and do all the things he liked or always wanted to do. How does a workaholic use retirement as a segue into oblivion? Especially when you retire from the most important part of your conscience; a life you loved that was the soul of your existence.

There can be no conventional "Golden Years" for Joe. Like a great river that feeds the estuaries, like any fountainhead, he must go on until he is no longer productive. Similar to the historic classical Roman General, Joe will probably be carried off the practice field on his shield of brown grass and churned up turf.

Only one thing could influence Joe to retire. And that would be if all his children were married and all began to produce  families. As the grandfather of a new breed that would need all the husbanding, guidance, and counsel in an unstable world, he would have a new priority. But for now, the "Lion" will continue to roar and hope for more grandchildren and another National Championship.

Joe Paterno doesn't play golf, doesn't like to fish, doesn't take pictures and certainly is not a horticulturist. The fact of the matter is, he has no hobbies. It's the price paid for being a workaholic with a zealot's desire to reach his goals. Joe  believes retirement is a waste of time. To get up in the morning not having something meaningful to do would be a slow death to this man. But as his grandchildren increase in number and age, he might finally find a satisfying hobby.

But for now, bring on the future! And let's hope for some more grandchildren!

# Chapter Twenty-four

# THE BASHING OF GRAND PA

The Lion King of 1994 would be wounded by a competitive predator in 1995. He could have retired after the '94 season and dwelled on his accomplishments. But challenging fate and that possible Roman General's demise he accepted 1995 as a new adventure and would be accompanied by his new grandson Brian.

The 1995 season would be a unique and eventful year for Joe Paterno and Penn State. A season that could be best described as historical and memorable in Joe's life.

JoPa finally became a Grandpa. His oldest daughter, Diana, had her first child, a boy named Brian Armstrong. Boy, was Joe proud and happy! Diana delivered on a Saturday morning before the Purdue game. In an earlier chapter, I had mentioned that many modern day women weren't eager to have children and wanted careers. I think Diana had Joe worried, but now he was ecstatic with his new grandson. That was the highlight of 1995. But the season would also have an abject low point, possibly the nadir in Joe's career.

In 1994, the Penn State team went 12-0, but once again was deprived of a National Championship. With a win over Miami, Nebraska who had been rated number one, was declared National Champions. There would be no playoff against number two Penn State.

So entering 1995, the Penn State players and of course their coach were caught between the trappings of disappointment as a segue to confirm their 1994 achievements. The Lions had the longest winning streak (17) in the country and they wanted to prove sophistic pollsters wrong. However, from the bridesmaid '94 squad, three players were drafted number one within the first nine NFL picks. The combined contracts of Ki-Jana Carter, Kerry Collins and Kyle Brady exceeded $40 million (with bonuses). Obviously some people realized how good those players were and how good the '94 team was.

When a team loses three offensive players who are first-round picks and an All Big-10 Center, Bucky Greeley, one would expect a drop off in performance. In 1994, Penn State had broken all the Big 10 and NCAA offensive records. But the fans and so-called pundits expected a repeat in '95. Besides the loss of four outstanding players on offense, Penn State would have a new inexperienced quarterback in Wally Richardson. Moreover, State's opponents had a full year to devise new defenses to curtail the '94 juggernaut.

Defensively, the Lions had lost all their first-string linebackers and lacked experience at the downline position. And two of their best young newcomers, impact players Floyd Wedderbern and Brandon Short, suffered season-ending injuries. Yet naive fans anticipated another Big 10 Championship and a possible undefeated season.

Joe tried to tell the fans and the public not to expect too much from the '95 squad. Sure, they had some fine players returning in Engram, Hartings, Rivera, Johnson and Conlin, but there were just too many uncertainties.

Texas Tech, who won the Southwest Conference in '93 and played in the Cotton Bowl, would be Penn State's opening opponent in '95. Joe warned everyone that Tech had a fine young squad with great speed on defense. They loved to blitz and had an All-American LB in Zack Thomas. Joe proved to be correct. Texas Tech's defense attacked Penn State aggressively, using a variety of blitzes that would have caused problems for a veteran quarterback, let alone the inexperienced Wally Richardson.

Penn State beat Texas Tech, 24-22, winning with a characteristic late fourth-quarter drive. But the game would be a strategic prototype of how opponents would play Penn State for the remaining season; blitzing defenses with a short underneath passing game on offense.

In the second game, State easily beat an outclassed Temple squad, 66-14. Fans remained steadfast, saying Texas Tech was just "a wakeup call". But the trained eye could see the Lions had some problems. The offense lacked the finesse and cohesion of '94 and made repeated mental errors. The quarterback was inconsistent and the tailback position had become decimated. Stephen Pitts, slated to be the starter, had injured his foot and would be out until the Michigan game. Mike Archie tried to pick up the slack but needed help. A great prospect, Ambrose Fletcher, was suspended pending a court decision. So Joe had to switch freshman linebacker Curt Enis to tailback. Enis had been a runningback in high school and would turn out to be a pleasant surprise in '95.

Rutgers would be Penn State's third opponent in a game to be played at the Meadowlands in New Jersey. The game would terminate competition between the schools. Since 1984, when Rutgers declared it intended to be a top power in the east, a climate of acrimony began to develop. Rutgers alumnus Sonny Werblin, the music mogul and former owner of the New York Jets, was the driving influence.

But no matter how much money Werblin poured into the football program, it remained on a treadmill. Although Dick Anderson, a former State offensive coordinator, seemed to be making progress (he upset Penn State in '88), he and Werblin clashed and Anderson was released. Joe Paterno rehired him as a quarterback coach. The way "good guy" Anderson was dismissed lacked class.

Following Anderson, smooth-talking Doug Graber was hired. Graber had a reputation as a good recruiter and stated he intended to get the best New Jersey players for Rutgers.

And as promised, he did get some fine players. But he also publicly declared that Penn State's days of recruiting top Jersey boys were over. Somehow the Lions continued to recruit well in the Garden State and Graber would never beat Penn State.

Coach Graber knew a win over Penn State could be a milestone for his program. In 1995, Graber would have some fine players, including All-American tight end Mark Batagllia, dangerous and talented quarterback Ray Lucas and two fine running backs in Willis and Presley (both named rookies of the year in the Big East Conference). Penn State's erratic performance, in the opening two games offensively and defensively bolstered Rutgers' confidence. Coach Graber also used the termination of the series as an added emotional incentive.

Penn State would have continued playing Rutgers if they would have agreed to play two games at State College for each contest in Jersey. The reason being that Penn State's stadium seats 96,000 and is always sold out. Even with the Lions as their foe, Rutgers would have difficulty drawing 50,000. So a home and home arrangement would be financially imprudent for State. Especially when so many other teams would be eager to take Rutgers' place on the schedule and would draw more fans.

By kick-off time, the acrimonious dialogue from Rutgers reached a crescendo. Rutgers was determined to win this game.

Two days prior to the game, Joe appeared on national T.V. and he criticized some of the top teams for running up the score due to pressure from the pollsters. In 1994, Penn State may have lost the National Championship by not running up the score against Indiana. The Lions had a big lead going into the fourth quarter, but Joe yanked all the starters and substituted freely.

Indiana was allowed to score three touchdowns in the closing minutes, the last TD on the final play of the game, cutting Penn State's margin of victory. The Nittany Lions were voted out of their number-one slot and dropped to number two based just on the score, and Nebraska assumed top ranking and rode it to a National Championship.

Little did JoPa realize the fickleness and hypocrisy of the sports media and some fans. September 23, 1995, would turn out to be one of the most disheartening experiences in Joe Paterno's illustrious career, even though the Lions won, 59-34.

Based on Rutgers' earlier games it would appear that Penn State's defense would have to contain their dangerous quarterback, Ray Lucas, who could run as well as pass, and the running game led by Willis and Presley. So defensive coordinator Jerry Sandusky structured the defensive game plan accordingly. Lucas started the game at quarterback and was playing with an injured ankle. Soon he would leave the game and not return.

Coach Graber had cleverly prepared a shot-gun offense similar to Florida State's but with a new quarterback, Higgins, at the helm. It caught the Lions completely by surprise. Instead of utilizing their fine runningbacks, tight end Mark Battaglia playing as an "H" back was featured. In football jargon, an "H" back is a tight end-type player who lines up in a slot formation and often goes in motion relative to the defensive alignment. Emphasizing the short pass to Battaglia, Rutgers was controlling the ball and matching Penn State touchdown for touchdown.

Fortunately for State, the Rutgers defense was as porous as their own, and the Lions began to pull away and had the lead going into the fourth quarter. But the Rutgers team refused to quit and remained dangerous. So it was only late in the game when Joe could chance multiple substitutions. With a few minutes left, State led, 53-34, and was playing with many substitutes.

The back up quarterback for Wally Richardson was a big redheaded kid, Mike McQueary. Mike had almost no game experience. Yet going into a tough Big 10 schedule, he would have to assume the quarterback duties if Richardson were injured. Every coach tries to get his backup quarterback as much playing time as is feasible. With time running out,

McQueary entered the game. State ran three plays and punted. But Rutgers, utilizing their time outs, stopped the clock and went on offense. Football teams are coached never to quit, so it was natural for Rutgers to try to get another score.

Four passes were thrown again, stopping the clock and turning the ball over to Penn State's offense. Now the scene was set for a cataclysmic ending that may have caused Penn State to lose their next game with Wisconsin.

A coach hates to tell a young quarterback who not only needs the experience but wants to show what he can do to kneel down on every play just because you're ahead. He gets no feel of the game and learns nothing. Consequently, Joe let McQueary hand the ball off as the clock wound down. But as fate would have it, approaching the last play of the game, Joe could have had McQueary kneel down or let him try to make the seven yards needed for a first down by throwing one pass.

There is a pass play in football that every team uses. It's designed to go to the tight end and is good in short-yardage situations. Joe wanted his kid quarterback to get the experience of completing a pass for a first down, and the game would be over. The play is designed to put a tight end to the wideside of the field and a split-end into the sidelines. The backs fake a run toward the tight end and he runs a route against the grain to the sidelines. The split-end streaks down the field to clear the area. The split-end is seldom open, as a normal defense would cover him first.

Probably because it was to be the last play of the game, the Rutgers defense, all eleven, lined up in the scrimmage area and just didn't move. When the controversial play was executed, the Rutgers defensive backs let the wide receivers run free. Therefore, when McQueary saw Chris Campbell, a substitute split-end running free 20 yards down field waving his hands, he did what he was coached to do and took his best option  and instinctively let the ball go. The play ended up as a TD, giving State six more points. The game was over and then the bashing of Grandpa Joe by the media became more important than the truth. St. Joe had finally made a human mistake in front of the American public.

At a game's end, it is common procedure for the opposing coaches to meet and shake hands. JoPa quickly ran to Coach Graber to shake and explain the last score was unintentional. Most coaches who saw what happened and were aware of Joe's record knew it was an accident. And I think deep down so did Graber. But he was frustrated. His team had played a fine game but didn't get the upset win. And with the termination of the series, he knew it was his last chance to beat Penn State.

As Joe extended his hand, Graber pulled back and snapped, "I didn't think you were that kind of coach" implying Joe deliberately ran up the score. The ESPN cameras had focused on the two coaches, but didn't include the assistant coaches in the background. Joe's initial response to Graber's comment was to turn on his heels and begin walking away. At that moment, a Rutgers assistant coach accused Joe of having a bet on the game.

Suddenly all the unjust criticism that Penn State had been receiving since they left the East and joined the Big 10 got to Joe. For the first time he lost his cool in public. When he heard the ludicrous, disrespectful remark by an assistant coach, he responded, "Bullshit!" At that time, another Rutgers assistant coach used a four-letter word. But the only thing shown was Joe Paterno using a barnyard epithet.

What subsequently transpired was an unjust bashing of one of the most distinguished coaches in history, and a journalistic mockery. Of course, ESPN had a field day with the scene, showing it over and over. But that was to be expected. It was the independent Eastern journalists and media (mostly with Eastern attachments) who violated every principle of professional journalism. They went beyond extrapolating. The entire incident was never investigated to reveal what actually happened. Only a one-sided, slanted view was taken by many Eastern writers and broadcasters. It was the opportunity they had waited a long time for. JoPa had slipped and shown a human side. They now had an excuse to sully and pillorize a man held in high esteem by the top coaches and educators in the country.

This was Howard Cosell journalism at its worst, blatant sensationalism based on fabrication. Before elaborating on some sickening examples written and said by people who never played any sport well, let alone coached any, it must be pointed out that the local N.J. paper that covered Rutgers football defended Joe Paterno. They implied Graber used the incident as an excuse for losing the game. And they reminded the public that a few years prior, Rutgers scored over 60 points against a weak Colgate team and were throwing passes in the fourth quarter. The Jersey paper was tired of Rutgers' poor records. Coach Graber would be fired at the end of the '95 season.

For using one minor profanity, one writer wrote, "Joe Paterno curses like a sailor on a weekend pass." Another wrote, Joe was a hypocrite for diving into the "muck of college football".

Broadcaster Mike Francesa, graduate of St. John's and honorary coach for Rutgers' spring game with his radio partner Chris Russo was the worst. He had the audacity and arrogance to defame one of football's all-time great coaches. Without trying to find the truth, Francesa implied JoPa was a classless hypocrite and was sure that Paterno deliberately ran up the score. Francesa's malevolence burst through his microphone. For years he had been wrong about Penn State. Now he could vindictively get his revenge.

WFAN, the sports radio show, had deteriorated to the level of the daily talk show. Many in the audience are dysfunctional sport buffs. It would seem the inmates are running the asylum.

Because he was angry at himself for losing his poise and using a barnyard word in public, Joe made a public apology for the invective. But he let his record speak for himself concerning the accusation of running up the score. Joe doesn't allow profanity in his house and I can attest to that fact, he enforces his beliefs. Like my father, Joe never swore. I did all the swearing for the family.

When I heard he was going on TV to apologize, I called and said it wasn't necessary. The people who attacked him were not that dignified to worry about. But he did go on TV and I could tell he was definitely upset. Joe knew he had many enemies, especially in the East. When you dominate the way Penn State did in the East, people get jealous and bitter.

Prior to the Rutgers incident, Joe seemed to be invincible. One writer, Ivan Maisel (*Newsday*), tried to find out what exactly happened and called Rutgers to speak to the assistant coaches, but was not allowed an interview.

The days after the Rutgers fiasco would harden to a tough week of practice. Wisconsin, the 1993 Rose Bowl winner, would be the Lions' first Big 10 opponent in their attempt to repeat as champions.

On paper, Wisconsin didn't seem to be one of the stronger Big 10 teams. They had a fine quarterback and were superbly coached by Barry Alvarez. Joe had to be careful the team didn't look past Wisconsin to the following week when they faced powerful Ohio State. Normally Joe would stay close to his team, constantly warning them of possible upsets. But Joe wasn't himself. The fiery taskmaster seemed to be in a fog. Some people who witnessed practice noticed his dismay and maybe the players did also. The man had been deeply hurt by the attack on his reputation and the embarrassment he and his family had to endure. A team is an extension of the coach's personality.

Penn State played lethargically and listlessly against Wisconsin. Maybe they were looking ahead to Ohio State and maybe they also were suffering from emotional despair. Wisconsin won the game, 17-9, and there went State's chance for a repeat trip to the Rose Bowl. They regrouped, but lost a close game to undefeated Ohio State, 28-25 in the final minutes.

But Joe and the Nittany Lions weren't about to roll over and die. Personally, I thought the Rutgers incident hurt Penn State for one week but aroused the players and challenged their resolve to have a good season. Penn State would win all the remaining games except Northwestern, the Cinderella team. Northwestern would win the Big 10 and a trip to the Rose Bowl.

The strong finish by State won them a trip to the Outback Bowl to play Auburn, the number-two team in the Southeastern Conference. In the latter part of the season, Wally Richardson improved with every game and by season's end had accumulated statistics that surpassed Kerry Collins in his junior year. And the defense really came on, so by Bowl time, the Lions were playing well on both sides of the ball.

JoPa and his team closed what would have to be called a bizarre season with a resounding victory over Auburn. Auburn, coached by Terry Bowden, son of heralded coach, Bobby Bowden of Florida State, had broken every offensive record in the school's history. But Penn State, led by Wally Richardson's splendid performance (similar to Kerry Collins' virtuoso vs. Tennessee in 1993) and an aggressive, relentless defense, easily handled the Tigers. At season's end, Joe and his team survived the "hurt" from the Rutgers game and finished with Penn State class.

Over the years, Joe had been anointed with many sobriquets, but in 1995 he finally got the one he wanted most, "GRANDPA."

# Chapter Twenty-five

# 1996—THE BEAT GOES ON

The 1996 season turned out to be one of the most rewarding and memorable in Joe Paterno's fabulous career.

JoPa turned 70 on December 21, 1996. He didn't have much time to celebrate, as he was getting his team ready for the New Year's Fiesta Bowl versus the University of Texas.

For Penn State to be selected in an Alliance Bowl game after surviving some shaky periods during the season in itself was rewarding.

But even more exciting than that, Joe had become a granddad again six months earlier. Joe's youngest daughter, Mary Kay, gave birth to a beautiful little girl (Olivia). Now Joe had a grandson and a granddaughter and renewed vigor. Forget about retirement.

As the '96 season approached, Penn State didn't look very strong from a personnel basis. Gone to the NFL were the two superb wideouts, Bobby Engram and Fred Scott. Both fullbacks, Whitman and Milne, would also make NFL rosters; as would tailback Mike Archie. But the biggest void on the offense would be the line.

Three players from '94-'95 were first-round draft choices: Kyle Brady, Andre Johnson and Jeff Hartings. And the remainder of the unit, Bucky Greeley, Marco Rivera and Keith Conlin would also become NFL players. Almost all of the above had played two or three years for Penn State. So who would be left to build a strong unit for '96 and give freshman sensations Curt Enis and Aaron Harris enough daylight to unleash their skills?

The defense looked a little bit more seasoned but had suffered a huge loss when outstanding defensive end Brad Scioli tore his knee cartilage. And the highly touted prospect, defensive tackle Floyd Wedderbern, was slowly recovering from a knee injury. Brian Noble and Chris Snyder had experience in the trenches but would need to greatly improve. Gerard Filardi would return at middle linebacker, but the outstanding Terry Killens was drafted, and Jim Nelson would have to repeat his 1995 performance as a linebacker.

The only strong area on defense would be the secondary with the experienced talented cornerbacks Tate and Miller and a great free safety in Kim Herring.

But the entire defense lacked depth. To compound all the existing problems, an early game was scheduled versus the highly touted University of Southern California in the Kick-Off Classic. When Joe agreed to play, I thought he was tempting fate. Many experts had picked Southern Cal to win the National Championship. And John Robinson, their head coach, had said he had a great squad. Even though Penn State had an outstanding quarterback coming back in Wally Richardson and a lot of talented freshman, no one gave them much of a chance vs. the University of Southern California (including me).

In fact, most people felt it would be a long year for Penn State in the Big 10. But Byzantine Joe had a plan and once again surprised everyone, maybe even himself.

The Kickoff Classic was to be played in Giants Stadium at the Meadowlands in New Jersey on August 25, 1996. By the NCAA rules concerning preseason practice, Penn State would be allowed 25 pregame practices, meaning the players would have to give up most of their summer vacation. But true warriors never pass up a chance to compete against a highly talented adversary. Also, they would quickly find out how good or bad they were and what needed to be fixed.

This '96 squad would make history, becoming the only recruited class to win four major bowls played on New Year's Day. That accomplishment was achieved by a team made up of 28 freshmen; 16 true freshmen, 12 redshirts, plus 16 seniors, many with minimal experience.

You could call 1996 a bookend season, opening with a dominating win over favorite Southern Cal, and closing with a dominating victory over favorite Texas, who had won the Big 12 by crushing the University of Nebraska. What happened in between was an adventure in pride, determination, hard work, mutual love and respect and courage by the players. And the teaching and coaching performance by JoPa and his staff could be called the envy of any coach—college or professional—who ever put on a pair of those old coaching pants.

Approaching the Southern Cal game, the Penn State offense was showing signs of stability and improvement. The wideouts, Jurevicius and Nastasi, showed indications of being impact players. Quarterback Richardson continued to throw as he did in the last five games in 1995, and the backfield of Enis, Harris, Chris Eberly, and Jason Sload and freshmen Chafie Fields and Cory Mitchell had depth.

So everything hinged on the offensive line. Starting the Southern Cal game, the only offensive linemen who had considerable experience were center Barry Tielch and Pete Marzyck at tackle. But senior Jason Henderson and newcomer Brad Davis were improving, as was Ostrowski.

Penn State dominated Southern Cal and seemed much better prepared, both physically and strategically. Enis had a great day, breaking the Kickoff Classic record for rushing with 167 yards. Richardson and the rest of the offense looked sharp. The defense played solid, if not spectacular. But it just looked too easy. Regardless, the Penn State fans became ecstatic and the pundits voted State #3 in the polls.

The Blue and White would have almost a three-week layoff before the season opener at home versus the University of Louisville. And then adversity struck. Just when the offensive line seemed to be stabilizing, Jason Henderson was diagnosed with a broken foot, an injury requiring six weeks to two months of rehabilitation. And Brad Jones, the man playing next to him, developed a serious blood clot that would finish him for the season. One side of the line had to be patched up in a hurry. But how?

Outstanding freshmen Karel Smith and Basin Grant were also out for the year. Bill Kenney, offensive line coach and JoPa put their heads together and made some desperate changes. Offensive tackle Pete Marcyzk was moved to guard, and true freshman John Blick became a starting tackle. Inexperienced sophomore Eric Cole was moved to the other tackle to back up Bill Anderson.

Kevin Conlin, the back-up center, would also have to play guard. How long would it take this revamped group to get the necessary timing and discipline and learn their assignments would be anyone's guess.

Having an experienced solid quarterback with competent receivers and backs would mean nothing if the offensive line couldn't protect the quarterback and open up some running lanes.

On September 7, 1996, Penn State would play Louisville for the first time at Beaver Stadium. Although coach Howard Schnellenberger had gone, he left a legacy of excellent players. Penn State would have to be alert. It was an eventful weekend, as 95,000 fans showed up, ignoring the remnants of Hurricane Fran.

Maybe the honoring of the 1986 National Championship Team motivated the adventurous crowd. The Nittany Lions beat Louisville 24-7 with a dominating defense and special teams. The Cardinals had five turnovers and only managed 50 yards rushing. Curt Enis had another big day with 104 yards rushing in a relatively easy win. It was Penn State's fifth consecutive win. It was the defense's turn to dominate while the offense was adequate, almost the reverse of the Southern Cal game, but the score was the same, 24-7.

In their third game, the Lions would score an easy 49-0 victory over Northern Illinois. Joe had had an opportunity to play many of the freshmen, as Penn State led, 35-0, at the half.

Definitely a solid team effort, but it was against a 1AA squad. Certainly not the caliber of a Big 10 team. However, one could notice the Blue and White defense beginning to really come together. Although not big compared to most of their opponents, they had good team speed and played a smart, stunting, swarming style. As always, Coach Sandusky had a good game plan.

Penn State continued to win easily with a 41-0 win over pesky Temple. It was the first time since 1978 that the Lions had consecutive shutouts. Again the defense and special teams were outstanding. The Lions' tight ends, Cuncho Brown and Keith Olsommer, had five receptions and it seemed the offense was about to regain a better balance between the run and a pass. But were the victories over Louisville, Northern Illinois and Temple a true test of the strength of the squad? Was the Southern Cal win a fluke?

On September 28, 1996, the Nittany Lions would make their first visit to Wisconsin since 1970. After silencing a noisy crowd by taking a 17-3 lead, the Lions faltered, and Wisconsin tied the game, 20-20, with 3:22 left to play. But "Captain Comeback", Wally Richardson, got the Lions in field goal position with 1:23 left, and Bret Conway kicked his third field goal for the victory. This was a young Wisconsin team that figured to get better. But the following week would be the real test. Penn State was 5-0 and would play Ohio State in Columbus. The Buckeyes were playing offense like Penn State did in 1994 and they also had a great defense.

The unbeaten Buckeyes were ranked No. 1 and had destroyed Notre Dame at South Bend. This was a veteran team on both sides of the ball. Could this youthful Lion squad with 26 freshman and only 16 seniors have a chance for an upset?

I and some of my associates from the radio show arrived in Columbus well before the team. We had a nice lunch and went back to the hotel lobby to wait the arrival of the squad. I couldn't help thinking about how many of the Penn State freshmen were playing on high school fields the year before. And now they were to meet a tough veteran team ranked number one in the biggest TV game of the day. It seemed surreal.

The Lions arrived Friday afternoon, and as the squad came into the lobby to get their assigned rooms, the silence was palpable. Coaches like squads to be serious and somber, intensely focusing on the game. But there is always a mix of some joviality and youthful vibrance; the Penn State squad seemed to be almost dormant. I began to get the same feeling I had in 1994 before the Illinois game. This team seemed to be in a mental funk and some of the freshmen were too uptight. I made that remark to Fran Fisher and Frank Giardina, and they both agreed.

Although Penn State played almost error-free ball, they were soundly thrashed by Ohio State, 38-7. Certainly Ohio State was the better team, but the Lions seemed lethargic and outclassed. Were the Buckeyes that good or did the magnitude of that game get to this extremely young squad? Some of the young players were too tentative in their execution.

Not only was the Lions' eight-game winning streak snapped, but a seed of doubt was planted concerning the rest of the schedule. Penn State could only accumulate a paltry 211 yards compared to Ohio State's 565 yards. The following week would be Purdue, and State would be home for the first time in a month. Using tailback Enis as a receiver (seven receptions for 94 yards) the Lions whipped the weak Boilermakers, 31-14. It looked like JoPa had the boys back on track.

A good Iowa team would be the next foe, and with Northwestern, Michigan and Michigan State still to play, the Lions needed a win if they were to stay in the hunt for the Roses. Iowa did not play well. They had only 268 total yards, only eight first downs, had nine penalties and had to punt nine times. However, Penn State let the game slip away as the offense was a little inconsistent and unable to make big plays.

Maybe the '96 squad lacked that killer instinct. Iowa won the game, 21-20.

Pesky Indiana would be up next in Bloomington. The Nittany Lions played their worst first half of the season, trailing 20-10 at halftime. Indiana moved the ball at will against a Penn State defense who was being outcharged and outhit. I could almost read Joe's mind. Now was the time to find out how good some of his young players were. JoPa would substitute freely in the second half. The Lions received a deserved tongue lashing by the veteran coach.

The second half became the crucible for the remainder of the season. Suddenly there was a galvanization of youth and experience, pride and leadership. Mike McQueary played for Wally Richardson and Chris Eberly subbed for banged up Curt Enis. They sparked the Lions in a spectacular second-half comeback. The defense allowed the Hoosiers just two first downs and 31 total yards in their first eight second-half possessions. A rout was on. JoPa's boys tallied 38 points to only 6 for Indiana in the second half. It was an unbelievable turnaround. The old man had not lost his flare for magic. It was the team's best performance since the Southern Cal opener. Players were getting comfortable in their positions and many of the freshmen had grown up in a hurry. This was Penn State football.

The Cinderella team of 1995, Northwestern, conquerors of the Lions and Rose Bowl participant would be next. The '96 Wildcats squad was playing like they did in 1995 and were ranked in the top 10. They also had a 13-game winning streak over the Big 10 teams. It would be a full-house crowd braving the weather with sporadic snow bursts and a national T.V. audience. Northwestern would be the perfect foe to test the quality of the Lions' strong showing against Indiana.

Considering Southern Cal's weak '96 showing, Penn State's performance against Northwestern had to be their best effort of the year. Their rejuvenated play in the second half against Indiana became seminal to a continuum of superlative execution against the stunned Wildcats. Led by the newly and invigorated defense and quarterback Wally Richardson,

Penn State routed Northwestern, 34-9, and snapped their 13-victory winning streak against Big 10 opposition.

Northwestern completed a 73-yard touchdown pass in the fourth quarter but was held to less than 17 points for the first time in 1996. Quarterback Wally Richardson was 11-22 for 201 yards and Curt Enis rushed for 167 yards. It was a truly dominating victory. Next up was Michigan at Ann Arbor and the Lions would have a week off to get ready to try to beat the Wolverines three consecutive times.

JoPa was a happy man. Happy with his new granddaughter Olivia, happy with the way his team was developing, and happy that on the weekend of November 8, he and I were to be inducted with our 1949 teammates into Brown University's Athletic Hall of Fame.

On Friday, November 8, Joe was to speak at an alumni luncheon in Pittsburgh and then fly to West Hampton, New York, to pick me up. Both of us were looking forward to seeing our old teammates and friends and trading some lies. Suddenly the reality of life abruptly halted our plans. Joe's father-in-law, Augie Pohland, passed away while Joe was at the luncheon. So JoPa immediately left for the Pohland home in Latrobe, Pennsylvania. Naturally, we didn't make the Hall of Fame dinner.

August Pohland's death awakened the ghost of my inner self, "Larry". Although Augie was in his early 80s, I reflected back to the day my dad died at the age of 59. Both men were of similar character with similar personalities. What great friends they would have been.

At least Augie got to see his children married and have grandchildren. The world needs the family-oriented establishment people like Augie and Joe who maintain morality and who can improve life within the parameters of contemporary society. But the world also needs the "Larrys" who believe in the same values but function outside of the establishment's loop. If humans are to survive and civilization is to improve, we need the dreamers like Larry and the doers like Byzantine Joe.

The task of preparing for Michigan snapped Joe out of his despair. The Lions had consecutive wins over Michigan in 1995 and 1996. And not too many teams had beaten the Wolverines three times in a row and twice in Ann Arbor. Another strong performance by the blue and white would mean a young team was not young anymore.

It would be week 11 and the last away game. A win over Michigan would put the Lions in position for a major Bowl. The first half ended with Penn State holding a 13-10 lead.

Michigan regained the lead, 17-13, with 12:52 left in the third period. But the Lions came roaring back. In Michigan's next six possessions, they turned the ball over five times and had a punt blocked for a touchdown. Curt Enis ran for 100 yards, putting him over 1,000 as the stunned Michigan crowd saw their team lose for the third consecutive time to Penn State. Michigan State would be next, and a win was absolutely necessary to gain a major Bowl bid.

It would be a typically scripted Penn Sate versus Michigan State game—exciting, close with a dramatic ending. It was a scintillating 32-29 win as the 16 seniors performed in outstanding fashion to give JoPa his 17th 10-game winning season and would result in a major Alliance Bowl appearance against powerful Texas.

Once again, All-American Bret Conway converted a clutch 30-yard field goal with 12 seconds left to give the Lions a smashing victory. Conway and his classmates posted a 41-7 win-loss career record, tied for the best four-year mark under JoPa. "Captain Comeback" quarterback Wally Richardson was outstanding in his final game. Wally was 21 of 31 for 281 yards and a touchdown. But most important, he guided the Lions to fourth-quarter score. With 4:27 seconds to go and the game tied 29-29, Richardson directed an 11-play 67-yard drive to set up Conway's winning field goal. Statistically the game was very even, but Richardson's performance along with Joe Jurevicius' eight receptions for 117 yards plus Curt Enis' 165 rushing was the difference. Coach Saban of the Spartans had to be frustrated as the Lions beat Michigan State for the fourth time in a row. Against two of the Big 10 powers in the state of Michigan, Penn State is 7 of 8. The victory set up the year's bookend victory against Texas and a number seven rating in the polls.

JoPa has indicated he will coach until he is 75. Boy, are the records going to fall. A highlight for "Larry" was an article printed in *Sports Illustrated*. The author kept implying Joe and I are very different people. I convinced him we had the same ideals but used different methods in postulating and sharing them. Joe was a pragmatic idealist operating within the establishment and I was the romantic idealist and dreamer operating out of the loop. The author decided I was an eccentric independent with a  free spirit. I guess he's right. The article was well received and many people told me that they identified with me and even though they were not famous either, they had productive, good lives. We all can't be heroes.

# Chapter Twenty-six

# HEROES

A ll animal groups have leaders and so does the species homosapiens. In primitive cultures, leadership was based on who was the physically strongest. But as man's brain developed, leadership was decided by a mix of brains and brawn.

As society continued to evolve toward civilization, leaders became heroes, and a psychological need for these heroes became evident among the masses. A hero figure represented a commonality for people of similar tribes—Great Warriors were the prototype of early heroes. But as civilization evolved and governments were formed and countries developed, heroes became more diversified. Besides warrior heroes, political heroes began to emerge, and with the advent of the printing press, authors also became part of the hero milieu. In the late 20th century, the star athlete has emerged as the new version of a hero, probably a psychological spin-off of the warrior general.

Admirers of the elite group we call heroes often give blind allegiance, exaggerate accomplishments and are willing to forgive minor imperfections in their favorites.

Unfortunately, not all heroes are good people. The printing press, radio and TV have provided the technological means to influence the thinking of the masses and create spurious hero figures who manipulate people. As with Hitler, Mussolini, Stalin and others, politicians with feet of clay often perpetrate fraudulent characters to constituents. And the favorite heroes of kids—sport celebrities—have been falling off their pedestals by the score. When people can no longer have and believe in heroes, there is a negative reaction that disseminates distrust and despair through society.

Why are the Joe Paternos, Joe DiMaggios, Joe Louises, Ted Williamses, Walter Paytons, and Michael Jordans necessary? Because they are authentic symbols of quiet dignity and great achievements. But we can't have a world of only heroes who have achieved fame and fortune. It's the common, everyday person who will shoulder the future of mankind. Napoleon once said to some of his pompous generals that the most important person in his army was the infantry man (foot soldier), because he pulled the trigger and made the difference in battle.

So for all of you who are related to or are close to a famous person and his or her great shadow becomes heavy like cement, remember that the hero can't be successful without help. To live according to one's beliefs in a humane way is just as rewarding as being a famous person. A man is the sum total of his living experiences, not necessarily a product of changing morals and mores. People who participate in the Peace Corps and other humane societies are the true heroes. Believe me, I know that there is a rewarding place for the "Larrys" of the world. Christ and every great leader needed foot soldiers to interact with their fellow men. I will continue to be "Larry" and Joe will continue to be the "Lion King."

If Joe had one final wish, he would like to replace St. Peter at the gates of Heaven and be present at the "Last Judgment". When the final decision of Heaven or Hell is made, Joe would like to run a two-minute drill for all the souls who might not get into the "Big House."

# MORE PENN STATE TITLES